LOST IN TRAINING

First published in 2008 by

WOODFIELD PUBLISHING LTD
Bognor Regis ~ West Sussex ~ England ~ PO21 5EL
www.woodfieldpublishing.com

ISBN 1-84683-066-4

LOST IN TRAINING

*The final hours
of Lancaster L7575*

HARRY GREEN

Woodfield

Woodfield Publishing Ltd

Woodfield House ~ Babsham Lane ~ Bognor Regis ~ West Sussex ~ PO21 5EL
telephone 01243 821234 ~ e-mail enquiries@woodfieldpublishing.co.uk

Interesting and informative books on a variety of subjects

For full details of all our published titles, visit our website at
www.woodfieldpublishing.co.uk

*To the memory of the
5,327 officers and men
killed in RAF training accidents
during the Second World War.*

'He noticed a movement and as he bent down the young man rolled onto his elbow holding his head in his hand.

Dad remembered the shock of dark hair falling over the man's hand. He was trying to say something. It was a woman's name. Though very quiet, Dad heard it twice, quite distinctly:

"Eileen, Eileen".

Then with a deep sigh the young airman sank back to the ground and lay still.'

Jean Arnold

~ CONTENTS ~

ACKNOWLEDGEMENTS

It wasn't easy writing a book about an aircraft accident when all the crew were killed. Your principal witnesses, the ones who knew what really happened, were not there to tell the story. The same problem applied when recounting their life before enlisting and their subsequent training. For this reason, it would have been an impossible task without the help of witnesses in the St Albans area, aircrew who underwent the same kind of training and several ground crew who were there at the time. Another very big problem involved finding the relatives of the crew after more than sixty years. This was especially true of the two older members, the pilot and navigator who were in their thirties and unlikely to have any surviving siblings. It took many months to find the navigator's next of kin and I never found the pilot's. Fortunately he was from the Royal Australian Air Force and their service records are now open to the public. Furthermore, the RAAF photographed their entrants and kept far more details than their British counterparts. As for the rest, I was fortunate enough to find their relatives, even the Australian Rear Gunner's, by one means or another.

The writing of this book has been a long voyage of discovery. Starting with a service number on the back of a pocket chess set, sent home amongst my cousin's possessions after he was killed, it has been a slow process, a gradual accumulation of information, one discovery leading to another. The first problem was trying to locate the crash site from the ambiguous information on the accident card. For most of this early research I owe a huge debt of gratitude to Brian Warren, Honorary Archivist of Potters Bar Local History Society. He found the crash site, visited the farm nearby, spoke to the present occupants, took photos and put an advert in the local post office that was answered by one of the main witnesses, Phyllis Gregory. Being in the farmhouse when the aircraft came over, she provided the kind of information that only one so close to the crash site could have known. Hers was the only family in the village permanently affected by this tragic event when her mother died a month later, having never recovered from the shock of what she had seen.

Another important witness was Bob Robinson who had a graphic story to tell and whose contribution helped to define the aircraft's route and what happened to it on its last fatal dive. Vital was the evidence of the late Enid Roberts, told me by her daughter Nancy Taffs, and most of all, the testimony of Jim Butters. With his knowledge of aircraft, he was able to construct a likely sequence of events from when he first saw the bomber up to its final moments. Also, by comparing his observation of the aircraft that night with that of other witnesses, he was able to reconstruct the likely course of the Lancaster in much more detail.

For the history of the plane, Lancaster L7575, I owe most to ex-RAF Stan Bacon who searched tirelessly through his vast library of books to provide me with detailed information, and researcher Liz Evans did a fine job at National Archives to give me all the data I needed on squadron records and more besides. Sebastian Remus in Germany conducted a thorough search of Lufwaffe records, though unfortunately, not many of these survived the War.

But, I couldn't have written the book without the expert knowledge and experiences of surviving air and ground crew. The pilot, Ross Blanchard RAAF, navigator Jim Logan RCAF, bomb aimers Bert Cole RAF and Bill Pearson RCAF, and wireless operator/air gunner Norman Jones RAF were indispensable. Other aircrew who helped were pilots Peter Langdon and Bill Eames, whilst amongst the ground crew, were Allan Jones, who serviced L7575 and Cyril Hedges, who remembered my cousin when they started training at Blackpool.

Malcolm Jones, Allan's son, brought me up to date with the derelict state of the airfield at Wigsley with his comments and photographs, and supplied me with much further information concerning his father. Chris Wilson, a cousin of Bruce Davies, interpreted the Meteorological Office reports, Geoff Paine and Cyril Tedman made special trips to National Archives on my behalf in the early stages and Bill Chorley gave me the benefit of all his experience in air force research. Other ground crew include Des Evans with his tribute to Ted Porter, and Alan Cook contributed his father's experiences in the rescue services at Upper Heyford, whilst Lester Stenner told me of his father, a chief flying instructor at Wigsley. Bill Blanning has always been a mainstay with his books and information. I've received help and photographs from Sue Hobson and Christine Taylor in Australia and valuable advice from Hans Grimminger in Germany. Mr D.A.E. Morris first uncovered for me the fateful entry about the crash in the training unit's records and Ken King added further information concerning night fighter squadrons. Mark Pardoe was the expert on Metropolitan Police records, Angela Ladd on the German translation and Tony Lack, ex-wartime RAF, cast his critical eye over the text and proof-read the book for me.

An amazingly good response to an appeal in the Herts Advertiser brought forward a significant number of witnesses, several of whom have already been mentioned. Jack Last, whose father found the flying boot whilst out poaching, Marie Wren, whose father was one of the fire service at the scene, Linda Storey, whose mother from the local ATS searchlight unit was one of the first there, Jean Arnold, whose father, a bus driver, was off duty but hurried to the scene to help, Jean's husband, Bob, Bernice Chuck, Cynthia Turner, Peggy Winch, Jim Wild, Harry Harrop, John Carpenter, Len Bean, Jimmy Whiting, now the local licensee, and John Day, whose father was the village policeman, all contributed in one way or another. Harry Harrop, one of the latest to come forward, has taken a keen interest and contacted a number of potential sources on my behalf.

Most recently, a further appeal, this time in the St Albans and Harpenden Review, brought forward Bill and Joan Surridge, Jim Bacon, Arthur Allen, Keith Canfield, Phyllis Wilmot, Derry Pickering, Ed Kean, Ralph Howell and David Ansell, who has contributed some excellent illustrations. Another appeal, this time in the Welwyn and Hatfield Times, brought forward Brian and Pat Hayward, who contributed information and took photos, and also Peter Jervis, Jim Parker and his friend David Willson, who sadly lost his sight due to a V1 flying bomb explosion in 1944. Mention here must also be made of one of the most important witnesses, Ted Stebbing, discovered by Brian Warren. Ted was the first to hear the plane and included it in his book, 'Diary of a Decade'.

The details of L7575's crew would not have been possible without the kind cooperation of their relatives who allowed me to see their service records and lent me their photos to copy. Catharine Cheesman, the aunt of Bruce Davies and the most senior of my correspondents, has been outstanding in her encouragement and support together with her two sons, Andrew and Rob. I owe a big thank you also to John Thwaite's brother, Bill, and Mabel Cooke, sister of Albert Rooks. Peter and Martin Joannides, nephews of Eddie Stock, and Christina and Mary Williams, nieces of Eric Williams were too young to know their respective uncles, but told me all they could. Other relatives or friends include Peter Williams, John Hume, Harry Braithwaite (John Thwaite), Stephen Rooks (Albert Rooks), Norman Home and Peter McDonald (Bruce Davies).

The following people helped me whilst trying to find relatives: Aparna Ravaliya, the Sea Wing Flying Club, Southend, Tim Wood-Woolley, Lyn Housden and Gavin Archer of Debenhams, Southend, Edwin Rooks and Caroline Rooks. William Jones, Malcolm's brother, Peter Last, Jack's brother, Helen Spencer in the Lake District, Libby Davies in Adelaide and ex-RAF Peter McKeown, who gave me his Wellington Pilot's manual, also deserve my thanks. In the final stages of the book, I am particularly indebted to Steve Snow for his map drawing, and to my son Richard for his computer skills.

Besides these personal contacts I must mention a number of repositories whose records were indispensable to this book. Again, I note individuals who were particularly helpful:

- *National Archives of the United Kingdom*
- *National Archives of Australia (Dr Christopher Clark)*
- *Bundesarchiv – Militärarchiv (R.Bars)*
- *Ministry of Defence, Air Historical Branch (L.C. Morrison)*

- *Royal Air Force Personnel Management Agency (Miss D. Purveur)*
- *Royal Airforce Museum, Hendon (Darren Cowd)*
- *Commonwealth War Graves Commission*
- *Archives and Local Studies, Hertford (Anita Wilson)*
- *H.M. Coroner, West Hertfordshire (Margaret Jarrett)*
- *Barrage Balloon Reunion Club (Peter Garwood)*
- *Leeds Local Studies Library (Michele Lefevre)*
- *The General Register Office*
- *The Church of Jesus Christ and Latter-day Saints*

It's been my good fortune to have met and corresponded with some wonderful people. Indeed, it would be quite impossible to mention all the individual kindnesses I've encountered during the writing of this book. It hasn't been easy for relatives of the deceased to recall their loved ones, nor easy for me to ask some necessary questions that would remind them of their grief. But, I've been touched by their cooperation, by the kindness of the local people in Hertfordshire and the help I've received from ex-aircrew when my repeated questions must have tried their patience to the limits.

The brave survivors of wartime Bomber Command are indeed a remarkable bunch. There's a marked quality about these men that is difficult to define. But, if you compare photographs of a young aircrew volunteer from the time of enlistment to the time he gained his stripes, a year or two at most, you see the rapid transition from boy to man. They had to grow up quickly. There wasn't time for niceties. Training was tough. You either made it or you didn't. These men made it. They lost so many of their friends, but, somehow, they survived. They are a dwindling race and I have been so lucky and privileged to have made their acquaintance.

1. An Introduction

With the War finally over an exhausted nation could breathe a sigh of relief. Servicemen returned home, POWs were repatriated and though there would be food rationing for years to come, people could get back to some degree of normality. It was a time when crowds were delighted to see the return of their sporting heroes on cricket and soccer fields: a time when even an ordinary county cricket match would attract a large crowd to see the likes of Len Hutton or Denis Compton.

But, we were living in a very run-down Britain, the scars of war still all around us. As a child I can remember travelling through London in filthy trains on dusty seats of torn upholstery, looking out at the stark skeletons of bombed out factories and churches, and peering into the rooms of deserted houses half demolished in the Blitz. Here a living room, there a bedroom, with the wallpaper partially ripped off, even sometimes with the remnants of furniture: it felt like intruding into the private life of a family that had once lived there, that had once called that broken house their home. One time, when we got out at Waterloo Station, the workmen were high above in the roof, chipping off the coats of blackout paint that sifted down in black powdery flakes on the crowd below. I shan't forget my mother's disgust as our clothes were getting covered in the filthy black dust.

Yet, despite the grey austerity of it all, there was a general air of thankfulness and especially, at Christmas. At last we could celebrate the festive season, a time for families separated by war to get together again. My grandmother was the centre of our family. She lived in the upstairs flat of a large house that had been divided into two. There was a railway signal just beyond the bottom of the garden and when it was raised we would wait expectantly for the train and wave to the passengers as it passed us by. At Christmas everybody came to the flat; uncles, aunts, brothers, sisters, cousins. They all managed somehow to squeeze round the table for dinner. Brandy was poured over the Christmas pudding and with the touch of a lighted match, magically burst into flames. Then, if you were really lucky, you might find a silver 'joey' (*threepenny piece*) in your helping.

After the meal everybody sat round the living room that had been decorated with paper chains the children had pasted together. The focal point was a large Christmas tree. There were no coloured lights to be had in the shops but with electricians in the family that was not a problem. A circuit of domestic light bulbs of various shapes and sizes had been made and painted in several colours. This was carefully spaced round the tree, which was then covered in various shiny baubles and draped in strips of silver tinsel to reflect its light. This tinsel was in the form of metallized tape and was available in reels at the shops for several years after the War. It was, in fact, RAF surplus. Known as "Window", the tape was about 1.5cm wide and cut into strips of a certain length. Bomber Command then dropped it on the run-in to the target in order to confuse the German radar.

The children were informed that Father Christmas was about to arrive and waited in hushed silence as they heard the sound of heavy footsteps clunking up the iron staircase that led to the outside door of the flat. There was a rata-tat-tat on the door and in he stepped. There he was, to our open mouthed astonishment, in full Santa Claus regalia. It was one of our uncles, of course, but he had disguised his voice well and we were completely taken in. Toys like most commodities were in short supply at that time but as he gave out the presents I was particularly lucky. Little did I know in my childish joy that my luck was the result of a deeply tragic event that had befallen our family.

My cousin, Tom, aged twenty-one, an RAF sergeant, was a wireless operator in a Lancaster bomber and had been killed in 1943 (*see photographs of him and the rest of the crew*). I can just about remember meeting him once, when, as a very young child, I was playing with a friend at the top of the little cul-de-sac where we lived. He must have been home on leave and I saw this man come up the road, say a cheery hello, and present me with a small paper bag full of ginger biscuits; my favourites. A shadowy figure in my memory, he towered over me in his RAF uniform, though he was actually only five foot three.

Tom's parents were the victims of misfortune. They had been bombed out of their London home in the Blitz, then lost their only child, and because he had no brothers or sisters, many of his treasured possessions were passed on to me. Over successive years I found myself at Christmas time in possession of a clockwork train set, various Meccano kits of increasing complexity, gramophone records and above all, a little steam engine that ran on methylated spirits.

Meanwhile, I had seen him at various stages of his short life in our family photograph album, including pictures of him in RAF uniform. At a much later age I was given a pocket chess set with his name inscribed on the back (*see photograph*), but had taken little notice of it at the time. My father told me that his bomber had returned from a mission over Germany but had crashed somewhere in England, and that all the crew had been killed. He surmised that possibly the aircraft had been damaged in some way and unable to give out a recognition signal. There was a suspicion that it might have been brought down by our own guns that had mistaken it for a German plane.

As I grew older, I became more intrigued by this mystery and eventually decided to investigate. Reading a booklet on RAF research I discovered that I would get nowhere unless I knew Tom's service number. It was then that I discovered that he had written it on the back of his chess set, first when he enlisted, and later, as a Sergeant. Further enquiries uncovered the real truth that Tom and his friends had never flown on a real bombing mission. In fact, with the possible exception of a "nickel raid", dropping propaganda leaflets in France, they had never left the country. They were actually on their last exercise at a training unit before being posted to an operational squadron.

I then found to my astonishment that during the course of World War Two: '5327 officers and men were killed and a further 3113 injured in RAF training accidents 1939-45'

('Bomber Command', Max Hastings). 5327 men, mostly young, and many not out of their teens, were all volunteers. Nearly all these casualties, save for a few instructors, had joined the Royal Air Force Volunteer Reserve after the start of the War and embarked on the rigorously skilful training programme necessary to fly the latest aircraft on the most hazardous operational duties in the war zone.

Most World War Two books on Bomber Command deal with the experiences of the men who went into combat. They usually skip lightly over their period of training. This book is different. It's the story of seven men who "never fired a shot in anger". They undertook all the trials and tribulations of training. They were about to enter the air campaign over Berlin in late 1943: a time when the casualty rate in Bomber Command was at its highest and when, in fact, many who trained with them lost their lives shortly afterwards. But, they gave their lives, just the same.

The War brought together men from different countries and different backgrounds: men who in normal circumstances would never have met. This is the story of seven such men, their family backgrounds, their training and how they eventually got together as a team to fly an aircraft. Because they are unable to tell us personally about their training, some of their contemporaries, who were in a similar situation and did survive, have helped to tell it for them.

There's the history of the aircraft they flew on that last night of their lives, Lancaster L7575, and the famous mission in which it had previously taken part. There's one of the ground crew who serviced it, another who was in the rescue services, and the indispensable role they played. The story tells of what the men did with their time off, on the bases, visiting the local towns and on leave. It tells of a village that for one dismal autumn night was struck with the horror of war to the eternal grief of one particular family and to the lasting memory of others. Then there's the mysterious cause of the accident. How far can we rely on the official report or was there an entirely different reason?

Finally, this book is dedicated to the unsung heroes of Bomber Command: the ones who died during the training process. They must never be a forgotten statistic. They gave their lives and should be remembered along with the rest.

This is the story of seven such men.

2.   The Pilot

On the 15th May 1940, Ewan Moore Taylor enlisted in the Royal Australian Air Force at Pearce, the air force base on the outskirts of Perth. He'd lived in Western Australia for several years but his roots were very far from there. He was born in South Kensington, London, on the 18th February 1913. His parents were both Scots whose families had moved to the South East in search of better livelihoods.

The large Taylor Family had gone down to London in the 1880s. Lachlan, Ewan's father, was an agent for a shipping company, a job that took him all over the world. Jessie, Ewan's mother, came from an altogether more rural background. The Macdonalds had moved down to Wales in the late 1870s where Jessie's father was a gamekeeper and then on to Sussex where he and his extensive family enjoyed his much improved position of farm bailiff.

Lachlan spent lengthy periods abroad and his family were often out there with him. At the age of two, Ewan accompanied his mother on a voyage from Liverpool to New York. Then again, early in 1924, aged eleven, he sailed with his mother and sister from Liverpool to Rio de Janeiro where he attended the Collegiate Armitage Militar. This was probably where he learned to speak Portuguese. In fact, by the time he enlisted he also claimed fluency in French, Spanish and Italian.

At some time during the course of his education he had also attended Muresk Agricultural College near Perth, Western Australia, and Geelong Agricultural College near Melbourne. He was back in England in the early 1930s and by 1935 was a café proprietor. It was on the 14th March that year that he boarded the liner Balranald in the Port of London bound for Fremantle, Australia. For the next two years he worked as a diamond driller in the gold mines of Kalgoorlie in Western Australia. Then in 1937 he moved further west to the little Wheat Belt town of Kellerberrin where he worked as a hotel chef. It was a good stopping off point for travellers on the route to Perth and no doubt, the hotel was conveniently placed for that purpose. He remained there for two years before he likewise completed the westward journey and enlisted in the armed forces at the Western Australian capital.

By this time, he was twenty-seven years of age and the records describe him as of fair complexion, blue eyes, brown hair and five feet nine inches in height. His progression into the air force was smoother than most. He simply changed uniforms, from that of a civilian chef to one of an RAAF cook. He spent a month at No.4 Recruit Depot and then till April the following year at Station Headquarters. During this time he'd moved up a rank from Aircraftman to Leading Aircraftman. He was then posted to No.5 School of Technical Training at Perth and later that April, to No.5 Embarkation Depot.

We shall never know exactly what caused Ewan to change his mind and take another career turn, but sometime during his six months at the Depot he decided to volunteer for aircrew training. In doing so he exchanged the comparative safety of an air force cook to one of the most dangerous front line jobs in the war effort. Six other men he was yet to meet were to make the same fateful decision that would cost them their lives.

He returned to Pearce on the 12th October 1941 where he was posted to No.5 Initial Training School to commence his aircrew training and on the 2nd December was accepted as a trainee pilot. Most of the young men who volunteered to fly were aspiring pilots but few were afforded the opportunity. It wasn't just potential ability that was required but qualities of leadership if you were to be the captain of a bomber crew. But, this was all in the future. First, he would have to study the basics.

In deciding to retrain he automatically dropped a rank to Aircraftman. At this stage most of the training was of a general nature and all on the ground. All the trainees, including those who were studying for the other aircrew positions were still together and sharing in lessons such as mathematics, navigation, map reading, meteorology, astronomy, aero-engines, armaments, aircraft recognition, theory of flight and airmanship. At the same time, physical training was not neglected. They would have shared in outdoor activities like cross country running, gymnastics and sport as well as parachute training and the inevitable parade duty, or "square bashing", as it was commonly known. However, they would have separated from time to time for more specialist tuition, which, in the case of pilots would have been in aerodynamics and the principles of flying. At the end of it all there were the inevitable exams at which Ewan was obviously successful.

After these fifteen weeks and promotion back to Leading Aircraftman, he moved to No.9 Elementary Flying Training School on the 5th February 1942. This was situated at Cunderdin, in the West Australian Wheat Belt, not far from Kellerberrin where he had worked before the War. Now, at last, after all those dreary weeks of study, was the moment he had been waiting for. He was about to step into a Tiger Moth, the standard initial training aircraft used by Commonwealth countries throughout the War. It was a single engine two-seater bi-plane with open cockpits. Ewan stepped into the rear seat behind the instructor. The system of communication between teacher and pupil, through a length of tubing, was effective in its simplicity. Over the first few days he would have been introduced to the basic principles of flying.

Normally, a maximum of ten hours of instruction would have been allowed for the trainee pilot to have sufficient ability and confidence to fly solo. By this time he was expected to be able to take off, complete a circuit and land safely on his own. Ross Blanchard RAAF, who survived the War to achieve the rank of Flying Officer, went through a similar course at the end of that year. He notes: 'this ten-hour limit was commonly known as "the chop rate". Any trainee who was "chopped" was given alternate training in other aircrew categories or into ground staff. I was one of the lucky ones, for I was sent solo after seven hours and five minutes training.'

Ewan was similarly successful and as the course progressed so did the demands on his ability, until after about fifty hours in the air he would have been subjected to a final test. In this he would have been expected to perform any manoeuvre in the flying manual asked of him. By this time a very high proportion of the original intake would have dropped out of pilot instruction, so it must have been of particular satisfaction to Ewan to be awarded a Grade 'A' in proficiency as he went on leave for a few days in early April 1942.

This was the stage where they assessed whether would-be pilots were to fly fighters or bombers. Those with the faster reactions tended to be fighter pilots but it wasn't quite as simple as this. A question of temperament was also involved. It took strength and endurance to fly a heavy bomber on lengthy flights over enemy territory whilst remaining constantly alert. Lapse of concentration could mean instant death for the pilot and the six men in his charge. In Ewan's case, age would also have been a factor. He was by now twenty-nine years old; well over average for aircrew. This, and potential leadership qualities would have been a determining factor in his case. But, above all, there was the question of supply and demand, and by early 1942 bomber pilots were a prime requisite, not only to replace mounting losses but to increase the offensive over occupied Europe.

The next stage for a potential bomber pilot was the introduction to twin-engine aircraft and Ewan was duly posted to No.4 Service Flying Training School on the 6th April 1942. This was at Geraldton, a major coastal town about 250 miles North of Perth. Here he was introduced to the twin-engine Anson Mark I. The Anson was the first monoplane and also the first aircraft with a retractable undercarriage supplied to the RAF. It started service in 1936 and by 1939 it was operating in both Coastal Command and Bomber Command. Already hopelessly outclassed by more modern aircraft it was soon withdrawn from operational duty and was used instead as a training aircraft for bomber pilots and crew. Over a thousand were exported to Australia before and during the War and Ewan was amongst the many RAAF trainee pilots to experience their first taste of flying a twin-engine aircraft in 'Faithful Annie' as it was affectionately known. Most seemed to find it a pretty solid and dependable crate but nevertheless, even by the standards of the time, slow, cold, noisy and primitive.

Ross Blanchard, who ended the War as a Staff Pilot Instructor and continued his flying career as a pilot in civil aviation, remembers, only too well, his many wartime hours at the controls of an Anson. 'In my book the Anson was the only real piece of junk that I ever flew out of about fifty-five different types in my logbooks. For example, it took about three moves to get the undercarriage set up for retraction, followed by about 150 turns of the crank handle to get the gear fully retracted. This bird climbed at about 85 mph, cruised at about 90 mph, was very noisy, had fixed pitch propellers and a very annoying amount of time was spent fiddling with the throttles to get the props synchronised. The air conditioning was very basic, for if the system gave a reasonable temperature in the cockpit, everyone else in the aircraft was either too hot or too cold.'

This point of view, from a pilot whose lifetime's experience of flying has included much more sophisticated machines, would be very different to that of a trainee whose sole experience had been in a Tiger Moth. Ewan now had to master the much more intricate problems involved in flying a twin-engine aircraft. There was a lot to learn. Apart from take off and landing there were the various manoeuvres in the air, instrument flying, air navigation, night flying, cross-countries and formation flying as well as flying at low level. Then there were the various emergency procedures such as flying with one engine feathered, forced landings, action in the event of fire and abandoning the aircraft. Meanwhile physical fitness was not neglected with PT, sport and drill on the parade ground. If time and results are anything to go by, Ewan did not take to the Anson as easily as the Tiger Moth. It was over five months before he gained his wings and promotion to sergeant with a Grade 'C' assessment. His service record notes that he was not recommended for a commission, but in any case this would have only been awarded to the chosen few at this stage of their training.

It was now mid-September 1942 and time to travel across Australia to Sydney for a last spell of leave with his mother before he reported to the RAAF depot at Bradfield Park where he spent a month awaiting embarkation. At some time it appears that his parents had separated and Jessie had come out to Australia, for it's noted on his service record that he was supporting his mother. During his period of training her address changed several times as she moved about, possibly, to keep closer to him. As she was now in the Sydney area she might have seen him for the last time as his ship set sail on the 17th October 1942. We can imagine her feelings, a mixture of sadness and apprehension, though she could not have known that her son had only another year to live and that she would never see him again.

Two months later, he was at No.3 Personnel Reception Centre in Bournemouth. This south coast town was a familiar place to new RAAF arrivals and the broken pier, concrete tank traps and barbed wire entanglements cluttering the sea front were a stark reminder that they were now in a war zone. The festive season, such as it was in drab wartime Britain, was fast approaching, and Ewan was granted a fortnight's leave that would have given him a chance to spend Christmas and New Year with his father in Bristol. Then, later, he had a week from the 30th January and another from the 25th February. In Ewan's case, being British born, it wasn't so much an arrival in the U.K. as a return and he must have had plenty of relatives to visit on both his father and mother's side of the family. Then, back at Bournemouth he was promoted to Flight Sergeant on the 17th March.

In all, he was at the reception centre from mid-December for three and a half months, which, coupled with the lengthy two month voyage, preceded by a month at the embarkation depot, constituted a good six months since his last spell of training. There isn't anything on his service record to indicate absence through illness or any other reason, but such periods of inactivity seemed to be a feature of the "all or nothing" nature of service life. The cause for such delay could probably be attributed to supply and demand, which will be discussed in a later chapter.

When eventually Ewan was summoned back to the training programme it was to No.3 Advanced Flying Unit at South Cerney in Gloucestershire where he arrived at the end of March 1943. He now had to get acclimatised to flying in European weather conditions, which was of particular importance to pilots who had trained in the much clearer skies of Australia. South Cerney was equipped with the twin-engine Oxford. More technically advanced and more responsive than the Anson, it was far more comfortable to fly and it became the ideal aircraft in its day for pilot training. When talking of the Anson and the Oxford, Ross Blanchard says: ' there is just no comparison. The Oxford was an extremely delightful bird to fly; quieter, faster, more manoeuvrable, gear and flaps operation motorised, and variable pitch propellers.'

The staff at South Cerney were highly skilled and dedicated pilots. They would have continued Ewan's training in low level flying and formation flying by day followed by take-offs and landings by night. He would have encountered for the first time the cloud, rain and fog of Northern Europe and the total blackout at night that made navigation so difficult. The course structure at the AFU was of a flexible nature. It allowed for trainee pilots to go at their own pace and Ewan did very well to successfully complete it within seven weeks.

It was now time for him to fly a twin-engine bomber and find a crew. This took place at an Operational Training Unit and so on the 18th May he was posted to 16 O.T.U. Upper Heyford, in Oxfordshire, where he began to form the crew who were eventually to make their final flight on the 22nd October that year.

3.   The Navigator

Eric Williams was the oldest in the crew of L7575. Aged thirty-three in 1943 he was a good ten years older than most of the men he was training with. Born on the 24th January 1910 in Chadwell Heath on the Essex side of London's outskirts, he was the fourth of five children and the youngest of three sons. According to tradition the Williams, a farming family, had come from Gloucestershire. His father, Henry, had settled in the London area and was in domestic service as a coachman and then a gardener. Later the family were to move to Manor Park, North London, where Henry was a fruit market sales-man. Eric's mother, Kate, daughter of Edwin Reynolds, was born in Hackney where her grandfather had come from the Isle of Wight to take over a dairy business employing fourteen milkmen, including his son, Edwin.

Nothing is known about Eric's earlier life, where he went to school or his standard of education. His oldest brother, Harry, must have done well, for he gained a university degree, and was in the Army during the War rising to commissioned rank. In order to attend university he would probably have gone to a grammar school or similar establishment to obtain the necessary qualifications. Whether his younger brothers, Frank and Eric, followed in his footsteps is not known. Frank's occupation before and during the War is still a mystery, but like Harry, he survived.

Eric, according to his service record, was a 'clerk' before he enlisted on the 28th March 1939. The only surviving photo-graph of him is too hazy to reveal much of how he looked but he was, apparently, five foot six inches in height, with brown hair, brown eyes and fresh complexion. His first unit couldn't have been more conveniently close to home, for he joined 909 Barrage Balloon Squadron. The headquarters of the County of Essex Barrage Balloon Squadrons 908, 909 and 910 were at Chigwell. 909 Squadron operated forty-five balloons in the East Ham area.

In the earliest stages of his training, Eric would have learned the theory of how barrage balloons were positioned to protect a target. His instruction would have included wire splicing and rope knots. He would have been shown how to operate a winch and would have experienced the difficulty of controlling a balloon in the air, as it had to be kept head to wind. At the onset of war in September he was still an AC2 (*Aircraftsman 2nd Class*), but by mid-October he was a Balloon Rigger with promotion to AC1 on the 1st November.

Officially, it needed ten men, including two corporals, to form a balloon crew. In practice, the job could be done by seven, but this would not allow for any time off for leave or further training. A typical day in Eric's life at this time would have started at 7 a.m. but been preceded by a spell of two hours on guard duty at some time during the night. They would have slept in a wooden hut equipped with cooking facilities. After breakfast, cleaning the billet and personal equipment including rifle, they would proceed with operational orders for the day. This might involve flying or bedding the balloons, altering their height or close-hauling them. Hauling them down had in the early days been very labour intensive but was greatly facilitated with the introduction of a windlass on the side of the winch. But, besides operating the balloons, there was plenty of maintenance to be done. One of the worst jobs was to seal the holes in them when the fabric was punctured. Balloon Riggers were given a pint of milk a day to combat the awful effects of fumes given off by the benzene solvent in the rubber solution used for the repair.

On 1st April 1940, Eric was promoted to Leading Aircraftman, which at around this time would have brought in a wage of about £1/8/0d (*£1.40p*) a week. Small though this seems, it would have probably been double what he first earned as an AC2. On the 9th August he went to No.1 Balloon Training Unit at Cardington, near Bedford, the Headquarters for No.30 Group, controlling the London Area. He returned to 909 Squadron on the 20th September and on the 28th was awarded 83% on completion of a Motor Transport Course.

Peter Garwood of the Balloon Barrage Reunion Club writes: 'often these were held for Balloon Riggers to make them capable of driving the winch lorries and the winch mechanism to launch and wind in the balloon. The winch lorry had two identical engines, one to drive the vehicle and one to drive the cable winch. Both were operated by use of a conventional clutch, accelerator and brake. They then were Balloon "Operators" in the real sense of the word'. This reclassification was duly acknowledged in his service record on the last day of October.

It was probably some time early in 1941 that Eric finally made the fateful decision to volunteer for aircrew, a decision that Ewan Taylor was to make a little later that year. A day's visit to Cardington on the 3rd June before returning to 909 Squadron was followed by a recommendation next day for him to be accepted for training as an 'Observer' (a term that was soon to be replaced by the more appropriate, 'Navigator'). He had to wait till the 11th August to attend No.1 Aircrew Reception Centre at Uxbridge, then not till the 20th September to start his training at No.1 Initial Training Wing. Like the Initial Training School in Australia this was ground based and of a general nature similar to that undertaken by Ewan.

Another Christmas went by and spring had arrived before he started to specialize at No.1 Elementary Air Observers' School on the 1st April. At last he was making some progress and would have undoubtedly started airborne instruction during his time there. He obviously did well enough to be assigned a place on the Commonwealth Air Training Plan and arrived in Canada on the 17th July. By the end of that month he was at No.31 Air Navigation School at Port Albert, Ontario, a few miles North of Goderich, on Lake Huron.

Not far from there, at No.1 Air Observer School, Malton, near Toronto, Jim Logan RCAF started a similar course in mid-September that year and we can gather from his experience the type of training Eric probably received. Jim writes: 'we received our flying instruction in twin-engined Avro Anson aircraft going on cross-country flights where we kept on course primarily through map reading. I recorded some 73 hours of daytime and 23 hours of night flying. In addition to air navigation we were required to get up into the nose of the aircraft and do some aerial photography. Ground navigation courses consisted of the following: navigation, maps and charts, magnetism and compasses, instruments, reconnaissance, aircraft recognition, meteorology, photography, signals both written and practical, and armament. We were trained to use the sextant and had to record a fairly substantial number of star shots viewing the night sky.'

This centuries old nautical device was of very limited value in wartime conditions and of no use whatsoever in cloud. Jim remembers on one occasion when: 'on managing to safely navigate back to base after flying mostly above 10/10ths cloud, we learned that one of our navigators became so hopelessly lost, and so I was told, the pilot was only able to establish their position by flying low enough to see the foreign car license plates in Erie, Pennsylvania. I suspect this may have contributed to that airman not being recommended for a commission after graduation! I graduated as a Pilot Officer with the "O" wing as a Navigator on 30th December 1942'.

Eric was awarded his brevet just over a month earlier. He had up till then been an LAC but was recommended for a commission on the 19th November. He was, according to his service record, officially a sergeant for one day, before his promotion to Pilot Officer. All this took place whilst still in Canada. He arrived in the U.K. a week before Christmas with much to celebrate and undoubtedly would have had a chance to spend some leave at home over the festive period.

Ewan had disembarked after his voyage from Australia on the 16th December, two days before Eric, and gone to the Personnel Reception Centre in Bournemouth. Early the following year, Jim Logan's ship had docked in the Clyde, then it took an eighteen-hour train journey for him to reach Bournemouth on the South Coast. Months later, Bruce Davies, the rear gunner had also ended up at a Reception Centre in Bournemouth. Whether Eric went to Bournemouth is not certain, but if he did, he would have been there at precisely the same time as Ewan, which raises the question of whether they first met there. They certainly had something in common. Of a similar age, they were both much older than the average crew personnel and were both still single. It's also possible that Eric met up with John Thwaite, who was to be the bomb aimer in L7575. He had returned from training in South Africa on the 23rd March 1943 and was at the same Personnel Dispatch Centre as Eric for nearly a month.

Eric spent nearly four months at the Reception Centre, even longer than Ewan, before being posted on to further training. But, the RAF didn't always allow such lengthy periods of inactivity. Jim Logan recounts how a number of them 'were posted for a month to the RAF Regiment in Filey, near Scarborough, to receive basic training on how to defend airfields under enemy attack'. He notes: 'I am glad we were never in a situation where we would need to test that knowledge!' It was, of course, just time filling and eventually, he continued with his training as a navigator.

Next stop for Eric was No.2 (Observers) Advanced Flying Unit at Millom on the Cumbrian Coast where he arrived on the 20th April 1943. Ross Blanchard was a staff pilot at No.2 (O) AFU in 1944: 'I did two weeks day flying followed by two weeks night flying with a crew of myself as captain, a staff wireless operator and three trainees: navigator, bomb aimer and wireless op. There were no lights allowed on when night flying, which was excellent for night vision.' The course was of particular importance to those who had so far trained in Commonwealth countries where the flying conditions were very different to those they would experience over Europe in the Blackout.

Eric did his four weeks at Millom and was about to enter the final stages of his training when posted to No.16 O.T.U. Upper Heyford on the 18th May. Two days later he was promoted to the rank of Flying Officer.

4. The Bomb Aimer

John Fisher Thwaite was born on the 11th September 1921 in the Lake District. His father, Fisher Thwaite, was from a local Cumbrian family and in 1883 had emigrated to Australia where he was employed by the Queensland Land Survey and Registry in the building of the railway running West from Brisbane. This ran through an area where with hard work and enterprise he was to set up a sheep station. Eventually, after a life of sheep breeding, he returned to Cumberland, but sadly, as a widower, his wife having died twelve days before he set sail. However, back in England he met and married Agnes Grieve, the niece of his Queensland neighbour. She was of a farming family from Ettrick in the Scottish Borders. They had two sons of whom John was the elder.

Forest Villa, their family home, was in a beautiful location, overlooking Bassenthwaite Lake to the North, Derwentwater to the South and the heights of Skiddaw to the East. It was the scene of frequent visits from relations and friends when John and his younger brother, Bill, were children. One occasional visitor was Mrs Beatrix Heelis, better known to the world as Beatrix Potter. From a wealthy London family, she had come on holiday to the Lake District as a girl and had fallen in love with it. Of particular attraction was Little Town, in Newlands Vale, with its two farms, vicarage and couple of cottages, and these formed the background to several of her beautifully illustrated tales. The Thwaite boys knew the stories well enough and Bill remembers, as a child, taking the steep pathway up from the cottages out onto the hillside and half expecting in his imagination to encounter 'Mrs Tiggy-Winkle' in her cap and shawl round the next corner.

By the time the boys knew her, Beatrix was in her later years. Of sturdy figure, good height and greying hair, on her visits to the Thwaites she invariably wore a large jacket, a full-length skirt in thick grey-blue tweed and always, a hat. An imposing character, she was a great champion of the Herdwick sheep, a local breed famed for their hardy resilience to the Lake District terrain and weather conditions but of inferior value with regard to their wool. This was a bone of contention between herself and the boys' father who was in favour of crossbreeding to improve their yield.

As the boys grew they were witness to a dramatic event when in June 1930 their mother invited some Scottish friends down to stay. On Friday the 13th, the visitors were taken down to Lake Windermere and boarded one of the many boats lining the shore. Henry Seagrave was about to break the world water speed record in his craft, 'Miss England II'. Aboard with him were an engineer and an official from the Rolls Royce Company. They made a brilliant run across the measured mile in both directions averaging 98.76 miles per hour. Unfortunately, Seagrave didn't realise he'd broken the record and took his craft to the upper end of the course for another try. The mad screaming roar of the engines rose to an excruciating height as the boat suddenly swung round and leapt out of the water. The Thwaites and their friends looked on in horror to see the three-man crew flung from the cockpit. Boats rushed to the rescue. They found the drowned body of Hallwell, the Rolls Royce man, still clutching a pad and pencil. Seagrave died shortly afterwards in hospital. Willcocks, the engineer, though severely injured, was the sole survivor.

In the decade before Europe was yet again plunged into war, the two boys had to complete their education. For this they went to Keswick High School. Harry Braithwaite, who ten years later volunteered for air crew and completed a tour in Halifaxes, was Bill's age and can still vividly recall their daily cycle ride to school along the country lanes into the town. He remembers John as a 'bit of a loner, a tall slim lad who always cycled on ahead'.

John Hume, who later joined the Army and was also a fine rugby player, was in John's class: 'I lived in town but he cycled, regardless of weather, the two and a half miles to school. Consequently, we rarely mixed socially, but I do recall he was a most difficult person to tackle at rugby. He was a bright lad in class; much more able than I was.'

In fact, Bill also testifies to his brother's academic ability saying that subjects like Latin caused him no problems. It isn't surprising, therefore, that John scored well in his examinations. After sixth form he went to work for the District Bank (later to merge with the National Provincial, which subsequently merged with the Westminster). He started at the branch in Cockermouth and was almost immediately shouldering more than his fair share of responsibility. The manager, who had an addiction to alcohol, was frequently absent, and when he did attend for work, was helping himself to the bank's funds. Inevitably, the police arrived to remove him and John was left in charge until a replacement could be found. This, of course, all counted in his favour. He moved on to the Ambleside branch and then on to head office in Manchester where he went out with a daughter of one of the managers.

At this point in his life, the summer of 1941, John, approaching the age of twenty, made a decision. The bank realised his potential and were keen for him to attend university and take a degree. Had he accepted their offer he would have avoided service in the armed forces until the final stages of the War. Instead, he volunteered for aircrew, having been assured by the bank that after the War he could resume his studies. On the other side of the world, Ewan Taylor in Perth, Western Australia, was also making a similar decision. Tom Green, in London, had already enlisted the previous May as a Wireless Operator and Eric Williams had been accepted for training as an Observer (*Navigator*) in June. The War was approaching the end of its second year and the Axis powers were still very much in the ascendancy. In Europe only Bomber Command were able to carry the fight to Germany.

John enlisted on the 9th August 1941. According to his service record he had brown hair, blue eyes and a fresh complexion. At an inch over six feet in height he was to be the tallest member of Ewan Taylor's crew. At interview he was siphoned off into the pilot/observer category. He completed his ground instruction at No.8 Initial Training Wing and was promoted to Leading Aircraftman on 29th May 1942 when he commenced training as a Second Pilot.

However, changes were under way. By 1942, Bomber Command had realised that to achieve greater bombing accuracy it would be necessary to create a new crew position, that of bomb aimer, or as it was officially called; 'Air Bomber'. The 'Observer', who navigated the aircraft, had also been responsible for releasing the bombs once the target was reached, but with the advent of more sophisticated apparatus he was finding it increasingly difficult to perform both functions. So, the previous post of 'Observer' in the new four engine bombers was divided into two new categories; the 'Navigator' and the 'Air Bomber'. The position of Second Pilot was abolished to make way for the Air Bomber and thus John found himself regraded.

He was chosen to join the Empire Air Training Scheme in which trainee air crew were given instruction at schools all over the Commonwealth and in late summer of that year found himself on board ship for South Africa. Eric Williams had arrived in Canada on a similar scheme the previous month. John attended a Navigation and Bombing School at Port Elizabeth and was billeted at the home of two kindly old ladies on the outskirts of the town. He progressed successfully through his course and was promoted to Sergeant on the 6th March 1943. He arrived back in Britain on the 23rd March and proceeded the following day to No.7 Personnel Despatch Centre where he was to spend two months. Eric was at the same centre during that first month, so it is possible that they met. If so, they were not to meet again till much later because he didn't become part of Ewan's crew till at the Heavy Conversion Unit when he replaced the original bomb aimer.

Meanwhile, he needed to practise his bomb aiming in European conditions and for that was sent on the 25th May to exactly the same unit that Eric had left the week before, namely, No.2, (O) AFU, Millom. There he would have undergone a similar course to Eric. It was then time to enter the final stages of his training. He was posted to No.28 Operational Training Unit on the 22nd June where he would have first become part of a trainee crew in a twin-engine bomber, probably a Wellington. He was there for exactly two months and then after a week's leave went to his final posting at Conversion Unit (*CU*) 1654 Wigsley on the last day of August. Whether the rest of his crew went with him is a mystery. All we know is that between the 31st August and the 22nd October, by an unlucky twist of fate, John was to replace Ewan's original bomb aimer.

5.   The Flight Engineer

Albert Rooks was born on the 23rd November 1923 in Leeds, the son of Ernest and Muriel Amy Rooks. He was the second of five children: three boys and two girls. His grandparents were licensees of the Blue Bell Inn, Glasshouse Street, Hunslet, on the southern side of the inner city; a street that no longer exists. His father, a colliery worker and later a bookmaker, was a keen sportsman both on the rugby field, where he'd played for a time in the professional league, and in the snooker hall where he'd won the Leeds individual and Yorkshire team championships.

Albert was not a bit like his father. His younger sister, Mabel, describes him as quiet, reserved, sensitive and deeply religious. He channelled his energies into the life of the local community both as a regular member of the local Methodist congregation, as a corporal in the Leeds Messenger Corps and as a sergeant in the 18th Company of the Boys Brigade in which he gained the much-coveted King's Medal. After leaving St Lukes School, North Street, he was accepted for a position on the clerical staff of the local colliery office. In such a "reserved occupation" he could quite easily have sat out the War in comparative safety but such an easy option would have been against his nature, which was to offer himself to the service of his country. Mabel summed up his character when she said: 'There's nothing he wouldn't do for others'.

And so, soon after his eighteenth birthday he volunteered for aircrew and enlisted on the 30th January 1942. Described in his service record as of fresh complexion with brown hair and brown eyes, his five foot eleven inches in height destined him to be one the tallest in the crew of L7575 abut also, one of the two teenagers who never lived to see their twentieth birthday. His two brothers had also volunteered, the elder for the RAF and the younger for the Royal Marines. Both survived the War.

Albert's ambition was to be a pilot and he was received for training as a Pilot or Wireless Operator. A medical examination the following day revealed imperfect eyesight, which ruled out the possibility of a pilot. Whether he received any training as a wireless operator is not revealed in his service record. He may, indeed, have been on standby until the summer when on 27th August he was accepted for training as a flight mechanic. This inevitably led to a posting at No.4 School of Technical Training at St Athan in Wales, the ultimate destiny of all would-be flight engineers. He arrived there on the 15th October. His sister Mabel doesn't remember him as being mechanically minded and it wouldn't have been an easy option for him.

Most flight engineers were recruited from ground crew. For example, Norman Ashton, who was eventually to fly on fifty-four operations in Lancasters and survive the War with a DFC, had joined the RAF as an engine fitter in 1940. Aged thirty and with two years mechanical experience behind him, he volunteered for aircrew and arrived at St Athan a month after Albert. In his book, 'Only Birds and Fools', he recounts how the huge hangar there was known as the 'Flannel Factory', fully equipped for courses on the heavy four-engine bombers in use at the time, the Stirlings, Halifaxes and Lancasters, as well as the Catalina and Sunderland aircraft used by Coastal Command. He mentions lessons on 'engine and airframe construction, hydraulic, electrical, fuel and compressed-air systems, engine handling, propellers, flight drills, oxygen system and repairs in flight'.

With Albert's lack of mechanical experience there would have been a tremendous amount to learn, but by the 16th April the following year, after much perseverance and hard work, he was ready to start his examinations. Like Ashton, he had been chosen to specialise in Lancasters, his course including a week's visit to the Avro Works in Manchester from the 5th-12th June. At this point in time, the pilot, Taylor, navigator, Williams, wireless operator, Green and mid-upper gunner, Stock had already been at 16 O.T.U. Upper Heyford for nearly a month, Davies, the rear gunner, had just disembarked after a lengthy voyage from Australia and Thwaite, the bomb aimer, having returned towards the end of March from his training in South Africa, was up at Millom on the Cumbrian Coast at 2 (O) AFU getting acclimatised to British flying conditions.

Finally, Albert was rewarded for all his hard work on the 19th July when he received his flight engineer's brevet and sergeant's stripes with an examination mark of 60%, a very creditable 'B' Grade. After a few days' leave he was the first, of what eventually were to be the crew of L7575, to be posted to CU 1654 Wigsley on the 24th July 1943. Davies had already met up with the other four at Upper Heyford. They arrived at Wigsley on the 5th August, so, by this time, six out of the eventual seven were at the same unit.

6. The Wireless Operator

My cousin, Henry Thomas Green, known as "Tom", was born in South-East London on the 3rd April 1922, the son of Charles and May Green. The Greens originated in the Norfolk Fens where, in the closing years of the eighteenth century, Tom's ancestors, John and Betty, were struggling to feed their numerous children from subsistence farming. Faced with poverty their sons journeyed south to seek apprenticeships and a better life in London. They settled on the south side of the Thames in Southwark and Bermondsey, a rapidly expanding area that afforded good opportunity for employment. Each son became established in a trade and their children succeeded them. In the nineteenth century Bermondsey was a centre for the leather trade. Tom's father, Charles, was born in a street off the Old Kent Road and had been apprenticed to his father, a leather dresser and dyer. However, when the business succumbed to foreign competition, "Charlie" or "Chas", as the family called him, had been obliged to seek a livelihood elsewhere. After gaining the necessary qualifications he worked for Camberwell Borough Council as a sanitary inspector punctuated by service as a Corporal in the Royal Army Medical Corps in Egypt during the First World War.

Charlie, May and their only child, Tom, lived in Peckham Rye. Tom was educated at Alleyn's School in Dulwich and went on to work for Lloyds Bank, where, by the time he enlisted he was a clerk in the Pall Mall Branch. It must be said that his heart was not really in the banking business, but, probably at his parents' insistence, he stopped on beyond his eighteenth birthday to complete courses in short hand and commerce etc. to complete his training.

He had always been mad about aircraft and had been an air cadet whilst still at school. It was therefore almost inevitable that he would volunteer for aircrew. He was called to attend No.11 Air Crew Selection Board on the 21st May 1941 at Lord's Cricket Ground where he was interviewed and given a medical examination. He was accepted into the Royal Air Force Volunteer Reserve as an Aircraftsman 2nd Class under training as a Wireless Operator/Air Gunner (*usually abbreviated to 'WOp/AG'*).

Tom was the "Tom Thumb" of the seven who were eventually to become the crew at Wigsley, being only 5ft 3ins in height. He was of pale complexion with brown eyes and dark brown hair. He had to wait nearly five months before at last being called up. On the 2nd October he took the train to Warrington in Lancashire where, at No.3 Reception Centre, Padgate, a large RAF depot, he was issued with uniform ready for his first posting. Four days later, he continued on to Blackpool where at No.10 Signals Reception Centre he started his training. There's a group photograph of him in his first class: thirty-five recruits under the watchful eye of Corporal Hunt. Through various enquiries I have identified the names of ten, three of whom undoubtedly survived and three were definitely killed. Most famous of the survivors was Nicholas Alkemade, who, as a rear gunner baled out of a blazing Lancaster at 20,000 ft without a parachute and survived.

Norman Jones, who finished the War in the Far East as a Warrant Officer flying in Wellingtons, had started the same course two months before Tom and has vivid memories of Blackpool. When war commenced the RAF requisitioned all the holiday accommodation, much to their owners' disgust. Blackpool landladies had to supply the lads with bed, breakfast and a cup of cocoa at bedtime. They had a pretty tough reputation and must have appeared rather fearsome to a typical young recruit who had never been away from home before. As luck would have it, Norman was treated very kindly in both the houses in which he was billeted. Tom may or may not have been as lucky during the months he spent at 87 Coronation Street.

Cyril Hedges, another wartime survivor, who served out in Egypt, Aden and the Isle of Socotra, was in the same class as Tom. He remembers: 'Training was in the town. In the morning we used to report to a local point and had to march to the classroom to learn Morse code and also take the tests at certain speeds, as we got better. If you didn't pass you could be transferred out and nobody wanted that. It was almost a disgrace, I remember, to fail.' "Morse Happy" was the description given to those whose nerves finally succumbed to all those dots and dashes. Casualties from such an intensive course, Norman Jones remembers, were referred to 'Feldmans Arcade' where shopping premises had been converted into a medical centre.

There was a lot to remember. Most important were the 'Q' Codes. These were three letter signals, all starting with the letter 'Q'. They were, in effect, a quick shorthand method of sending a message involving several words. Norman learnt his Morse code in the old tram sheds, converted by the RAF for the purpose, and he recalls Physical Training, which took place in the ballroom of Blackpool Tower. This last activity was not much appreciated by the proprietors who were apprehensive lest continuous pounding of servicemen's feet should damage the specially sprung floor.

After nearly four months that took him over the Christmas of 1941, Tom was ready to move on. He was posted to No.2 Signals School, Yatesbury, Wiltshire, on the 29th January 1942. Norman Jones described the type of training he was now to undergo. He said that trainees would try to attain a standard of reading Morse code at a speed of twenty-one words a minute but should attain at least eighteen. They also had the theoretical and practical work ahead of them. He continues: 'They had to learn how to operate all the radio equipment they might meet and this included not only that equipment designed for and used by the RAF but also that in aircraft supplied by the USA. Then there was the theory of electricity and radio to grasp, plus that of learning what part each component played in making a wireless transmitter or receiver work.'

On the 20th April 1942 Tom was given an average mark of 47% for his Trade Test exams. Norman says that although it might appear low, it was a high enough standard overall for him to continue with his training. He notes: 'it was policy at that time to send trainee WOp/Ags on to RAF stations where it was intended that they should polish up their wireless operating skills in the respective signals sections once they had passed the initial W/Op course. Tom was posted to RAF Detling, Kent, on the 30th April. He was there for four months until his next posting to No.7 Signals School at South Kensington in London's West End. This was where trainees were brought up to date on the full range of radio and radar equipment they might meet when on an operational squadron. As radar was very new in those days and, of course, very secret, the training was on its function, not on how it was made up. Basically, this training course saw the transition between WOp/Ground and WOp/Air. It was very important and lasted about twelve weeks after which Tom would have been sent home for anything up to three weeks.'

Unhappily, 'home' no longer meant Peckham Rye, South-East London, for Tom. His parents' house had been wrecked in the Blitz of 1940-41 and all their belongings destroyed. Fortunately they had escaped unhurt and been obliged to seek lodgings elsewhere. When Tom enlisted they were living in Guildford, Surrey, but later, my father found them somewhere in Farncombe. We were living nearby in Godalming, which was why Tom usually paid us a visit when he came home on leave. On this occasion he returned to duty on the 16th December when he was posted back to No.2 Signals School in Wiltshire.

Norman writes: 'He was at Yatesbury till about the middle of March 1943 to complete the WOp/Air course. This involved the airborne operating of receivers and transmitters including air to ground wireless direction-finding procedures. It would have been here that he was issued with his personal Flying Log Book and a study of that, if available, would indicate the type of work carried out.' Unfortunately, none of the logbooks from the crew of L7575 are known to have survived. Logbooks of deceased aircrew were held by the authorities until after the War when next of kin could claim them. Nearly all unclaimed books were destroyed in the 1960s.

'On the 23rd March,' continues Norman, 'Tom arrived at No.7 Air Gunnery School, Stormy Down, on the Welsh Coast near Porthcawl, and on the 24th he was promoted to Leading

Aircraftsman (*LAC*). This promotion was standard for all beginning an Air Gunners course, unless they were already of equal or senior rank. It was in line with the policy that the minimum rank for Air Crew at that time was LAC. The course that he and his fellow trainees were about to take was an abridged version of that taken by "straight" AGs, due to the assumption that WOp/AGs would only man a gun turret in an emergency. Tom achieved average marks of 77%, so his gun aiming must have been very good. At the end of their course, on 7th April, they went on parade to receive their AG's brevet and Sergeant's stripes.'

Tom then had another spell of leave. My father notes in his diary for Saturday the 10th April: 'Went to the allotment this morning and did two hours digging. As I was coming away I saw Tom who had come to meet me. He got home last night on four days' leave. He is now a Sergeant Wireless Operator & Air Gunner. I hope he will be alright but the casualties are so heavy.' On the 13th he noted: 'this evening very many planes have gone over. Some will be missing by tomorrow, I suppose. The young men fly over. They do not fly back.'

It is evident from this that the public were aware of the high casualty rate. In fact, over the previous month 583 airmen had died in just seven raids over Germany's industrial heartland, the Ruhr. On the Duisburg Raid of the 9th April the attrition rate was over 8% (*'Bomber Boys', Kevin Wilson*). If that continued a bomber crew would not last longer, on average, than about twelve operations. By now, the heavy four engine bombers, the Lancasters, Halifaxes and Stirlings had largely superseded the medium twin-engine bombers in the European zone as the RAF's main weapon of attack which meant that for every aircraft shot down, seven men were lost. The figures were mounting and it was evident from his next posting that Tom was destined for a British based squadron.

This was at No.4 Air Observers School (*AOS*), West Freugh, on the 13th April, which later in 1943 was renamed No.4 (O) AFU, (Observers) Advanced Flying Unit, and would have been similar in purpose to No.2 (O) AFU at Millom, where Eric Williams and John Thwaite were trained. Like theirs, Tom's training lasted a month, probably following a similar pattern to that described by Ross Blanchard, the staff pilot at Millom, with two weeks' flying by day followed by two weeks at night in blacked out conditions.

Finally on 18th May 1943, two years after he had enlisted in the RAF, Tom was to enter the final stages of his training when he was posted to 16 O.T.U. Upper Heyford, ready to join up with Ewan Taylor and the crew to train on twin-engine bombers.

7.   The Mid-Upper Gunner

Edward Percy Stock, known to his family as 'Eddie', was born in Harringay, North London, on the 6th January 1924. He was the youngest of the crew but only by a few weeks. Albert Rooks, the flight engineer from Leeds, had been born the previous November. Neither was to see his twentieth birthday. Eddie's origins can be traced back to rural Essex. His grandfather, born in the village of Stebbing, had married and settled in Epping and his father, Percy, the youngest of a large family, was a constable in the Metropolitan Police. Eddie was the younger of two children. Their mother, Nellie, died in 1935 and their father married a widow who brought the children from her previous marriage into the family home. The loss of their mother at an early age drew Eddie and his sister, Joan, closer together and the further loss of her brother in 1943 was a grievous blow to Joan, according to her son, Peter.

Eddie's obituary, in the Hornsey Journal reads: 'Ted Stock was educated at Stationers School where he was one of the most popular boys. He was very keen on sport and played in the school's cricket and football teams. Before joining the RAF he worked for the Prudential Assurance Company, Crouch End, where he was well liked and respected. He was on the committee of the Hornsey Youth Club and was also secretary to the North London Youth Table Tennis League.'

This active participation in the local community was matched by an equally active sense of humour. Peter's godmother, Phyllis Green, became a life-long friend of his mother, Joan, when they met during the Blitz, in an air raid shelter beneath Tottenham Lane. A local vicar used to visit the shelter to offer words of comfort to those who had taken refuge there and as Phyllis descended the steps one night she heard him preaching his usual sermon only to find on arrival that it was Eddie taking him off.

The course of Edward Stock's life was to change dramatically when he volunteered for aircrew. On the 15th December 1942 he went before No.3 Aircrew Selection Board at Lords Cricket Ground, the same location that Tom Green, the wireless operator, had attended nineteen months before, and was accepted for training as an Air Gunner subject to a medical examination. This took place on the 19th December, he was given a Grade 1 Medical Category and was accepted into the Royal Air Force Volunteer Reserve as an Aircraftman 2nd Class from that date. Little did he realise at the time that this fateful decision would allow him only ten more months to live. His total service lasted 308 days, the shortest of all seven men who were to be the crew of L7575.

His service record describes him as five foot nine inches in height with hazel eyes, dark brown hair and a fresh complexion. Two scars in the centre of his forehead were probably the result of a sporting injury. By this time the family had moved to Glebe Road, near Hornsey Railway Station and Eddie might have had the chance to see them briefly for what was to be his last Christmas before being posted to No. 14 Initial Training Wing on the 2nd January 1943. Here he would have received basic training, mostly of a general nature common to all aircrew positions, similar to that described for the pilot, Ewan Taylor, at his Initial Training School in Australia. It would certainly have included instruction on aircraft recognition. It was of utmost importance to be able to recognise all the types of aircraft, both friendly and hostile, an air gunner was likely to encounter. This was no easy task when viewing a plane from any angle, sometimes with its shape partially obscured. However, Eddie seemed to have coped well throughout his training, being assessed as a Grade 'A' in 'Proficiency' and a 'V.G.' (*Very Good*) under the heading of 'Character'.

The next stage of his instruction commenced on the 3rd April 1943 when he was posted to No. 1 Air Gunners School at Pembrey, near Llanelli, on the coast of South Wales. The following day he was promoted to Leading Aircraftman, a standard procedure for those attending gunnery school, as had been the case with Tom Green, the wireless operator, when he was posted to Stormy Down a few days earlier.

Amongst Eddie's photos is a picture of him and his class, probably taken when he started at Pembrey. There are two groups of fifteen men, each with a sergeant in charge. The sergeant in one group has a damaged left hand. The instructors at these gunnery schools were invariably men with operational experience, sometimes being rested after a tour, or recovering from injury.

Norman Jones attended a course at No. 3 Air Gunners School, RAF Mona, on Anglesey and described the type of instruction that Eddie would have probably received. Clay pigeon shooting with a twelve-bore shotgun gave them some experience of firing at a moving target. Then, when they started to fly they would have practised air to ground firing. Meanwhile, the importance of observation was stressed in fighter affiliation exercises when they would undergo a simulated attack from a fighter aircraft and had to warn the pilot to take evasive action. Of course, it was necessary to become fully acquainted with the .303 Browning machine gun, standard armament in RAF bombers. This included being able to strip it, clean it and clear it when it jammed.

The ultimate target practice involved shooting at a drogue towed by another aircraft. Each trainee's ammunition would be tipped in a coloured dye to identify the number of hits he'd made on the drogue. Norman recalls that five hits from two hundred rounds were considered adequate. When one time he managed a score of fifteen it was dismissed as a "fluke". The reason for such a low percentage was due to the problem of calculating the amount of deflection required to hit a moving target. Up to 1943, gun sights were relatively primitive. The gunner had to rely on a combination of instinct and experience. Naturally, some were better than others. A lad from the Western Isles in Norman's group showed obvious promise in the clay pigeon shooting. He knew all about 'taking lead', as it was called, i.e. knowing how to shoot ahead of a moving target so that it flies into the line of fire. On being complimented by Norman he replied that where he came from, unless he hit the target they would have had nothing on the supper table.

A second picture of Eddie was taken when he was awarded his brevet and sergeant's stripes, having successfully completed the course. This was on 15th May 1943. The group photo is inscribed '57 Course A/Gs' and is of the twenty-two successful candidates. On each man is inscribed his surname. At least seven of them can easily be recognised from the earlier picture and no doubt the others are there too but this allows for eight who either didn't make the grade or who had already transferred to other courses. Training was deliberately tough and designed to weed out those who were not prepared to make the effort.

On the 18th May, Eddie was posted to No.16 Operational Training Unit at Upper Heyford in Oxfordshire where he met the pilot, navigator and wireless operator to form the nucleus of a bomber crew.

8.   The Rear Gunner

George Bruce Davies, known by his second name, 'Bruce', was born on the 2nd January 1923 in Adelaide, South Australia. He was the only child of Edward Walford Davies, known in the family as 'Walford', and his wife, Effie Priscilla who lived in the leafy suburbs of Wayville. Peter McDonald met Bruce at Unley High School where they shared a common interest in music. 'I remember going to Bruce's home in Clark Street a number of times and met his parents who were keen sup-porters of ballet. In 1940 I went to Adelaide High School and so our lives tended to separate. I knew Bruce joined the Air Force in the same year as I joined the Royal Australian Navy and subsequently heard he had been killed.'

Catharine Mary Cheesman, Bruce's aunt, also testifies to this love of ballet. She still has her brother's 'Six prints of Ballet Girls by Daryl Lindsay, his pride and joy'. In fact, Bruce inherited a love of music from both his parents, his mother being a talented singer, but above all, from the Davies, a family of Welsh descent, from Oswestry in Shropshire. His great-uncle, Sir Henry Walford Davies, was one of the most prominent musicians in Britain during the first half of the twentieth century. He was a professor in the University of Wales where he did much to promote Welsh music and musi-cians. He held a similar position at the Royal College of Music and eventually succeeded Sir Edward Elgar as 'Master of the King's Musick' in 1934. He was, above all, a pioneer in the field of music broadcasting in the early days of wireless and was well known to the public for his talks on music. One of a variety of posts he held was as Director of Music to the Royal Air Force. Many an airman has paraded to the strains of the 'RAF March Past' and it must have been a source of pride to Bruce to know that it had been composed by his great-uncle.

Bruce's grandfather, Edward Harold Davies, went out to Adelaide in the 1880s. His career almost mirrored that of his younger brother, Sir Henry. South Australia had seen little in the development of the arts and Harold Davies spent a lifetime putting it on the musical map. He was Professor of Music at the University, founded the Adelaide Bach Society which he conducted for thirty years and was the driving force behind the South Australian Orchestra whose first performance he conducted in 1921. He was well known to the public for his wireless broadcasts and articles on music and he did his country an inestimable service in the late 1920s when he accompanied expeditions into Central Australia to record and transcribe Aboriginal folk music.

'A holiday cottage was built by the family at Port Noarlunga, about twenty miles from Adelaide,' Mrs Cheesman recalls. 'We moved out of town for the long holidays as soon as schools and university closed: so, it was all of January. Effie, · Walford and Bruce would join us when they could. Bruce used to enjoy many holidays down there, swimming, and even trying to surf on a wooden board: such a wonderful way to spend the summer.' As he grew older he met up with half a dozen other boys who went camping there and it was then that he met Ross Blanchard who like Bruce was to volunteer for aircrew. They were to meet again during the initial stages of their training and later in England.

After he left school, Bruce went to work as a pipe fitter and later as an apprentice for a manufacturing engineer whilst attending the School of Mines on Tuesday and Friday evenings for classes in Electric Welding and Mechanical Drawing. Meanwhile, he continued to enjoy his outdoor activities, playing baseball and tennis, and when the opportunity arose, yachting and swimming. His school exam results had been modest. As his aunt says: 'He was a very happy child, much loved by us all. Not really academic, much better with his hands, as witness the balsawood plane he made and sent home to his parents'. This excellent and detailed model of a Lancaster bomber is still in existence and shows a natural ability of craftsmanship, bearing in mind that it was not made up from a kit.

Bruce inherited an interest in aircraft from his father who worked as 'a mechanic repairing planes' at Parafield, the local airport. Mrs Cheesman adds: 'Bruce was so determined to fly because Walford, who was Air Force trained in 1918, just missed out on active service. My son Andrew vividly remembers a conversation he heard, with Walford desperately trying to convince Bruce to go for Ground Force rather than Flight Crew. Then Walf said to my husband: "You have a go at him, Johnny." But it was to no avail, 'he was not to be persuaded.' And so, on the 23rd May 1942, the nineteen-year-old youngster enlisted in the RAAF. It was a fateful decision. He had exactly seventeen months to live.

The records describe him as 5ft 9ins in height, with fair hair, fair complexion and blue eyes. At his interview the officer noted: 'very neatly dressed, fair hair, thickset, well mannered, seems bright and alert, I think he will make the grade.' He was accepted for training as an air gunner and was sent to No.4 Initial Training School at Victor Harbour on the coast, fifty miles South of Adelaide. It was here that he crossed paths briefly with his friend Ross Blanchard who had also volunteered for aircrew and been accepted for training as a pilot. Ross arrived there on the 18th July and the two friends shared the initial training for a couple of months. Bruce went home with a promotion to Leading Aircraftman and was posted on the 17th September to No.1 Wireless and Gunnery School at Ballarat, near Melbourne. During that autumn he spent three weeks in hospital for reasons unknown. He was then out in time to spend what was to be his last Christmas before his posting to No.3 Bomb and Gunnery School, West Sale, on the 8th February. He completed his training in Australia, received his Air Gunner's brevet and Sergeant's stripes on the 4th March and was ready to embark for Europe.

There's a family photo of him when he came with his parents and girlfriend, Carlien, to say his last goodbyes to the Cheesmans and their three young boys. Anxiety would not have been far beneath the surface of smiles for the camera. In the event, his farewell to Australia was a lengthy and tedious affair as he was shuffled round the coast from one embarkation depot to another. First he was at Mitcham, not far from his home in Adelaide, for most of March, then to Ascot Vale, near Melbourne, till the middle of April. They then sent him to Bradfield Park, Sydney, for four days before rushing him up to Brisbane. As his ship steamed out of port, Bruce said goodbye to his homeland. Like many a young Australian airman in the early '40s, it was to be a "forever" goodbye.

He arrived in England on the 3rd June and was sent to No.11 Personnel, Despatch & Reception Centre, Bournemouth, the following day. Although England was new to Bruce he had plenty of relatives there. Professor of Music, Harold Davies, Bruce's grandfather, kept in close contact with his brother, Sir Henry, and the English side of the family. On the 16th March he wrote to his nephew, John Wilson, a teacher at Charterhouse School and a fine musician, the following letter:

'My Dear John, Our oldest grandson, George Bruce Davies (Walford's only son) is now in the R.A.A.F. and may be sent to England. If this should happen I have told him to at once get into touch with you at Charterhouse: and you will bring him into contact with the family...He is a dear laddie...Love him: be kind to him: show him all you can. Your affectionate uncle, Harold.'

On the 22nd June, Bruce was posted to No.16 O.T.U. Upper Heyford where he was to meet Taylor, Williams, Green and Stock, who had been there since the 18th May.

9.   Teaming Up

It was the 18th May 1943. The sunny weather continued. The daily papers showed a map of the waterways in the Ruhr and Kassel with the dams that were targeted the previous night with reports of flooding and 'colossal' damage as a result of the famous 'Dambusters' raid. A new intake had arrived at 16 Operational Training Unit, Upper Heyford in Oxfordshire. This was the stage where the different members of a bomber crew first combined to train as a team. The present intake would be Course No.57.

For all the formalised rigidity of service life in the RAF a remarkably fresh and flexible system was employed in the method in which men that had been trained in the various specialities were brought together. Essentially the bomber crew were a team that had to live and work in a situation where their lives were constantly in danger. It was essential for each member of the team to do his job properly and each depended on the other. Someone's lack of vigilance, some-one's mistake, and all could be killed. In their wisdom the RAF realised that for men to work together as a team in such circumstances it was vital that they got on well with one another and what better way than to get them all together in one place, such as an aircraft hangar, give them a few hours to mill around and get to know each other and let them team themselves up. Men of like mind and temperament were attracted to one another and the result was far more satisfactory than if arbitrary decisions had been made on paper.

Sometimes the 'crewing up', as it was called, was a little more structured. Pilots would be assembled in one room and navigators would enter and each pair up with a pilot. Then the bomb aimers would enter to form groups of three, then the wireless operators etc., till the process was complete. In another system the routine was reversed with men from each trade assembled in separate rooms. The pilots would then go round selecting someone from each trade until he had a complete crew.

Sergeant Bert Cole, who was finally a Warrant Officer when demobbed in 1947, was at Upper Heyford during the first two months of 1943. He remembers his first two or three weeks, being taken up in a Wellington with a staff instructor to practise bomb aiming and then falling victim to a virus that found him in the hospital quarters. It was there that he was approached by a pilot who invited him to join his crew.

Whatever system was in force by the middle of May that year, it brought together four of the seven men who were to fly in the crew of L7575 on the 22nd October. By now Flight Sergeant Ewan Taylor, RAAF, was thirty years of age, well over average for a World War II bomber pilot. Perhaps it was this age factor that attracted him to Pilot Officer Eric Williams, the thirty-three-year-old navigator who was about to be promoted to Flying Officer on the 20th May. The other two were much more the usual age, Sergeant Thomas Green, twenty-one, with the shoulder flash emblem of sparks denoting a wireless operator and youngest of all, Sergeant Edward Stock, nineteen, with his air gunner's brevet.

At this point in time the other three who were eventually to form the crew of L7575 were elsewhere. Sergeant John Thwaite, air bomber, aged twenty-one, had completed his course in South Africa, returned to Britain and was about to start his training in the U.K. at No.2, (Observers) Advanced Flying Unit. This was at Millom on the Cumbrian Coast, and as it happened, conveniently close to his home area. Albert Rooks, Aircraftsman 2nd Class, aged nineteen, was still training to be a flight engineer at St Athan in Wales, whilst Sergeant Bruce Davies, RAAF, air gunner, aged twenty, was in the midst of a lengthy voyage from Australia to Britain.

Meanwhile, Ewan Taylor and his crew were about to be introduced to the Wellington Mark III. The Vickers Wellington, or 'Wimpy' as it was nicknamed, was by far the most dependable twin-engine medium bomber of the early War years. The airframe, designed by Barnes Wallis of 'Dambusters' fame, was based on the framework of the old airships, consisting of a geodetic network of intersecting strips of aluminium-alloy that formed an extremely durable structure. Such was its strength that the Wellington could soak up gunfire, from which other aircraft would have surely succumbed, and limp home with its crew of thankful survivors. The Mark III was equipped with Hercules radial engines and a rear turret of four guns. It was the mainstay of the bomber offensive over Germany in 1941 but it was gradually being replaced by the four-engine heavies and by 1943 was largely used in Europe for training purposes.

When in prime condition crews found it a safe aircraft to fly. Jim McIntosh, a Canadian pilot (*'Lancaster at War 2',* *Garbett & Goulding*) describes it as 'a squat, solid looking kite with the high tail being the most distinctive feature. It flew easily and had no bad habits; you just felt safe in it. The feature I remember best was the pilot's seat, the most comfortable of all. The furniture manufacturers would have a winner if they could copy it.' 'What always struck me about a Wellington,' observes a front gunner, Robin Murray, ' as soon as you got into it was the smell of the dope, and as soon as it started to move you got this sort of flapping noise. But it was a very comfortable aircraft to fly in' (*'Bomber Crew',* *Taylor & Davidson*).

Unfortunately the Wellington IIIs at Upper Heyford had seen many hours of service before they were assigned to training. Despite the best efforts of ground crews age and general wear and tear were beginning to take their toll. For example, during the fortnight starting three days before Ewan's and his crewmates' arrival, 15th-28th May, one pilot had to land on a single engine when the other had failed for no accountable reason. On the same day, another pilot had already lost one engine when the other started to fail forcing him to make a belly landing on the nearest airstrip he could find. A few days later there was more engine trouble resulting in the pilot landing at an airfield in the Cotswolds. After a further two days a tail wheel came off as an aircraft was landing. Then the inevitable casualty occurred when an engine cut out whilst a pilot was taking evasive action during an exercise. When the artificial horizon and directional indicator collapsed causing him to lose control, he ordered the crew to abandon and one of them received fatal injuries whilst trying to bale out.

Added to this were accidents due to pilot-error of which there were three during the same fortnight. Two were whilst landing when in one case the undercarriage collapsed and in the other, a heavy landing resulted in damage to the airframe. Then, when a Wellington swung during take-off, the pupil pilot throttled back and ran through a hedge, which likewise didn't do the airframe much good. Considering these aircraft had been battered by flak, tested to their aeronautical limits in violent evasive action from enemy fighter attack and finally subjected to rough treatment from inexperienced pilots, it isn't surprising that they weren't the reliable machines they had originally been. Those in charge at Upper Heyford did their best to cope with the problem. Accidents in June due to tyre bursts were looked into and there were none in July. Far worse was a fatal crash in June when the main plane of an airborne Wellington became detached. A similar accident in July 'resulted in a special inspection of all main spars and the fitting of new or modified wings to all suspect aircraft' (*Operations Training Book*).

The large number of accidents kept the rescue services on constant alert. Douglas Cook (*see photograph*) had enlisted in the RAF on the 11th Dec 1941. At the time he was serving his seven-year apprenticeship to become a master plumber, his apprenticeship being deferred until after the War. He was stationed at 16 O.T.U. from the 1st October 1942 until the 22nd November 1944 and was promoted to LAC on the 1st May 1943, shortly before Ewan and his crew arrived there. His son, Alan, remembers how he referred to Upper Heyford as a 'crash drome'. His father was employed as a driver by the RAF, at which he excelled, especially on heavy and articulated vehicles. Whilst at Upper Heyford he drove a number of these, including the fire truck and the Coles Crane. He also drove the huge 'Queen Mary' vehicles used to transport aircraft sections. Later, whilst serving with 238(T) Squadron, he would drive road trains all the way across Australia, from Darwin to the south coast ports.

Being part of the rescue operation exposed him to the aftermath of many horrific accidents. 'As a boy my father used to tell me about his experiences driving a fire engine and chasing the damaged bombers across the fields as they couldn't always stop due to having their brakes fail. A lot of the guys were dead when they pulled them out of their (often burning) aeroplanes. They had three minutes inside the aeroplane in their asbestos suits to effect a rescue. Ammunition would often be going off around them. He said he'd received burns to his own hands trying to get someone out.' It was a job that took courage and dedication.

The sight of some accidents would stay with him for the rest of his life. One such occasion was when they were called out on a warm night after a blazing hot day that summer of 1943. It was Tuesday the 27th July and Wellington X3792 was part way through a cross-country exercise when it landed at base and returned to dispersal. The rear gunner, 19-year-old Stanley Packham left his turret. As he sauntered round in the darkness to the front of the aircraft he failed to keep clear of the starboard propeller. It was still revolving and the blade severed his head clean from his body.

This terrible accident took place two days before Ewan and his crew completed their course. But, the question is, who exactly were in his crew? Nearly all the crews training at Upper Heyford were destined for Conversion Units to operate the four-engine heavies. For this reason the intake represented six out of the seven crew positions needed in a Lancaster, Halifax or Stirling. Theoretically only the flight engineer remained to be introduced at the Heavy Conversion Unit (*HCU*), though sometimes, as will be seen, this also applied to the mid-upper gunner.

By this time the position of second pilot had been phased out and the navigator's responsibility for dropping bombs given to the new category of 'Bomb Aimer' (more officially known as 'Air Bomber' or 'Bombadier'). Perhaps, because the second pilot had been displaced by the bomb aimer, both pilots and bomb aimers were given instruction in a Link Trainer. Bert Cole did fifteen hours on this piece of ground-based equipment, the ancestor of the modern Flight Simulator. The pupil stepped into the mock-up of an aircraft cockpit complete with all the controls and instruments. This was linked electronically to a set of controls operated by an instructor at his desk who would put the pupil through the process of flying an aircraft. It is therefore evident that at this time, bomb aimers were being given at least the rudiments of elementary flying in addition to their normal function. Bert later put this experience to good use when he would take over the controls of their Lancaster to give his pilot a brief spell of rest on the return flights from operations.

Part of the course at the O.T.U. would have involved flying to a bombing range and practising with small bombs designed for the purpose. So, there must have been a bomb aimer in Ewan's crew of unknown identity who may well have continued with them on to the H.C.U. at Wigsley. The situation with Ewan's gunners is also problematical. The Operations Record Book (*ORB*) at the O.T.U. records an intake of '32 A/Gs' and '32 MU/AGs' in May. It's therefore obvious that the output of trainees from the gunnery schools had already by this time been allotted their positions in the four-engine bombers for which most were destined. The fact that Wellingtons didn't have a mid-upper gun turret meant that gunners training for this position were obliged to man the Wimpy's front turret. The intake and output of 'A/Gs' and 'MU/AGs' when Ewan and crew were there over the May, June and July of '43 shows that the balanced intake in May was exceptional and that there were normally fewer mid-upper gunners. In June only 22 of the latter started training as opposed to 46 'A/Gs'. This would indicate that some Wellingtons were being crewed by five men rather than six, with just the one gunner in the rear turret. Such was the case with Bert Cole and this situation is borne out by the experiences of other aircrew that remember the mid-upper gunner joining them at the H.C.U.

It's not certain whether Ewan started his O.T.U. course with one or two gunners. Eddie Stock was obviously with him from the start but the gun position that he normally assumed is a bit of a mystery. Gunners usually kept to the positions in which they were trained and rarely exchanged places. Bruce

Davies was undoubtedly the rear gunner on L7575's fatal flight because his body was found in the tail of the aircraft. Stock was one of the five who were flung out of the plane when it crashed but must have been assigned the mid-upper turret that night. However, in the report at the end of October '43 the ORB for Wigsley clearly states that Davies was the 'M.U.G.' and Stock, the 'A.G.'. At the Inquest, Squadron Leader Porter, who authorized the crew's final flight, listed Davies before Stock when he read out their names and it was normal practice to list the mid-upper gunner first. Also, when the crew were mentioned by name in the accident report supplied by the Ministry of Defence, Davies was listed before Stock. On the other hand, Ross Blanchard, Davies's friend states: 'my impression of Bruce's position in aircrew was that he was a rear gunner'.

Arriving in Britain just over a fortnight after Ewan and his crew started at the O.T.U., Bruce Davies had spent nearly three weeks at the Reception Centre in Bournemouth before his posting to Upper Heyford on the 22nd June. Here, instead of the full-length course, he only spent just over five weeks. He, therefore, must have joined Ewan's crew either as an addition or a replacement.

Staff at the O.T.Us. were men who had active front line experience and ran their units more on a squadron-like basis. In fact, on occasion, O.T.U. crews still in the training process had been called upon to make up the numbers in large bombing raids over Germany. Ewan and the majority of his crew went through the usual course at Upper Heyford, lasting about ten weeks. At any one time there were four flights, 'A,B,C & D', in operation, whilst the latest intake were on a 'Preliminary Week'. Meanwhile, the course that had just finished were on a week's leave prior to posting. By the end of May, Ewan's crew were in 'A' Flight, at the end of June, in 'C' Flight and finally at the end of July, on their week's leave.

During the Preliminary Week there would have been introductory lectures. It was a chance for the new intake to get to know one another and the crewing-up process would have been encouraged. It was necessary for Ewan to be introduced to the Wellington III and to get accustomed to the cockpit layout, aided by exercises in the link trainer. Then, in the last week of May, the crew were in 'A' Flight and ready to start their airborne training. First, Ewan had to learn how to fly the Wellington and would have been taken by an instructor on a series of circuits, learning to take off and land, known in RAF jargon as "Circuits and Bumps". It's possible at this stage of his training, that only Ewan and the wireless operator, Tom, were involved.

The bomb aimer, Bert Cole, recalls that in late November the previous year, his pilot and wireless operator, though billeted at Upper Heyford, were doing circuits and bumps from a satellite airfield at Hinton-in-the-Hedges. His pilot, Lou Watson, said the food in the pupil sergeants' mess at Upper Heyford was awful. But, it happened that Bert and his fellow crewmen, the navigator and rear gunner had been assigned billets at Fritwell Manor, a country house nearby. Lou said he wasn't going to put up with the food at the base, so they all jumped on the crew bus and headed for the manor house. Bert and his two mates dashed upstairs with their kit where they were to be sleeping on hard mattresses, known in forces jargon as 'biscuits'. Then, they descended to a small coach house, where two ladies ran a little tearoom. Bert remembers: 'with the austerity of wartime food rationing, we could hardly believe our eyes. There before us was a feast the likes of which we had not seen since pre-war days: sandwiches, cakes, trifles, absolutely delicious. We tucked in with gusto, then, when we had nearly finished, we noticed some odd looks from the other aircrew present. The skipper looked up and suddenly noticed: "Oh my God, everything free tonight, it's the birthday of the canteen". We went to the lady at the counter and made our very sincere apologies, explaining that it was our first night at Fritwell. We offered to pay, but she wouldn't hear of it.'

To put them at their ease she offered to read their palms and what she said to Bert he will never forget, but what became of Bert and his friends belongs to a later chapter. Suffice it to say, it's unlikely the food at the pupil sergeants' mess had improved by the time Ewan and his crew arrived at Upper Heyford a few months later.

Once the training programme was under way and Ewan had the ability and confidence to take off and land, the instructor would have taken him further afield on a cross country exercise or they would concentrate on instrument flying. Eventually he would progress to four-hour solo flights and various members of the crew would have their own instructors on board. Eric would practise his navigation to various turning points on ever-longer cross-country routes. There would also have been flights to bombing ranges where they dropped small practice bombs and Eddie would have been taken on gunnery practice, firing at drogues.

By the end of June, in 'C' Flight, the training would have got tougher with low flying, night flying and what was known as "fighter affiliation". Navigating the night skies in all weathers over the European blackout would have been a very different experience for Eric after his training in Canada. Jim Logan RCAF remembers how his training in the use of the sextant was soon forgotten once he was taught how to operate 'GEE' at O.T.U. in England. With the Gee-box it was possible to guide the aircraft to a target in cloudy conditions with a much greater degree of accuracy. This ingenious device enabled the navigator to home in on radio pulses sent from three different home-based ground stations and steer to an exact position.

Fighter Affiliation involved a mock attack by a friendly fighter. The gunner's vigilance was of prime importance in warning the pilot of the impending attack as soon as possible. The pilot then had to fling the aircraft into a violent manoeuvre known as the "corkscrew". If performed correctly, the plane should then have resumed its original course, which was hard enough by day, let alone in the night sky where Ewan and his crew would be operating.

In addition to this, the crew had to be trained in emergency drills should they have to abandon the aircraft. Parachuting was obviously on the main agenda, but they might also have to survive a ditching, which involved handling a dinghy or life-jacket ("Mae West" as it was called) in the water. This was done at the swimming pool, whilst back at the base there would have been classroom lectures on German flak, searchlights and night fighter tactics. There was also the problem of high altitude flying and correct oxygen procedure.

Then there were evasion exercises. Harry Yates at a similar O.T.U. in 1943 relates how crews were dumped out in the middle of the countryside in the dark and had to find their way back to base whilst police and home guard were under orders to hunt them down (*Luck and a Lancaster*). It was all a bit light-hearted really, and certainly at Upper Heyford, not taken too seriously, because there, the exercise was voluntary. The ORB noted in July that the 'Evasion exercises have been well supported. Over sixty pupils ran voluntarily on the last one, but despite all their efforts the usual 50% were caught before reaching base.'

Crews were kept on their toes with regular physical training. They received swimming instruction and could take part in athletics. In the June report, the ORB notes that 'Athletic Training forms part of the P.T. Scheme and regular evening practices are held. Athletic teams from the Station have competed with great success at Dodington and Woodstock scoring more points than any other competing team. Tennis is played regularly by many of the Station personnel.' But, 'Station and Inter-Wing League Games have had to be curtailed because of the tennis ball problem.' (!?)

One of Ewan's final exercises could have been what was known as a "Nickel Raid". This gave trainee crews a chance to fly over occupied territory and face the real possibility of enemy fire. A Nickel Raid involved the dropping of propaganda leaflets, usually over France. Unfortunately the ORB for Upper Heyford doesn't record the names of the crews who took part so we can't be certain in which raid Ewan and his crew took part but the most likely one took place on the 24th July. The ORB records that 'three Wellington IIIs were detailed to drop Nickels in the La Fleche, Angers and Tours Areas respectively. The aircraft detailed for La Fleche abandoned its mission at Southampton owing to both engines overheating and brought its Nickels back. The other two aircraft dropped Nickels successfully in their allotted areas and returned safely'. So, did Ewan and his crew ever fly over enemy territory? We shall never know.

Their very last exercise from Upper Heyford probably took place on the 27th July, when 'Seven Wellington IIIs took part in a Command Bulls Eye Exercise. Searchlights were particularly active, there being no fewer than twenty-one instances in which aircraft were held in searchlights for periods of longer than one minute. Five simulated fighter attacks were recorded' (*ORB*). In this particular instance the book does not record the route but as a good example of the extent of such an exercise, on 28th May that year: 'Three Wellington IIIs took part in a Command Bulls Eye Exercise in which the route was Leicester – Llangollen – Stratford-on-Avon – Staines – Kew Bridge – Walton-on-the-Naze – Northampton, with I/R targets at Stratford and Kew Bridge.'

'I/R', short for 'Infra Red', was an ingenious method of simulating a bombing attack on a real target in blackout conditions without involving explosives or anything dangerous. Tony Lack, who trained in Wellingtons, remembers how they used a cooling tower at Northampton as their simulated target. An infra red light was situated on top of the tower. As the aircraft crossed the target the bomb aimer pressed the bomb release button synchronised with an infra red camera that would pick up the light if the aim was accurate.

Later that year, on 22nd October, when five crews took off from H.C.U. Wigsley on their final exercise, Infra Red Bombing was cancelled due to bad weather. It was an exercise from which only four crews returned, but all this was in the future. For the moment, Ewan and his friends had completed the penultimate stage of their training and on 29th July started a well-earned week's leave.

10.   Final Training

My father's diary for the 29th July 1943 reads:

> *'Blazing hot today. Tom called. He is on his last leave before he starts on his work as a W.O. on a Lancaster doing night bombing. Poor boy. Please God he may come through safely'.*

We know from Ewan Taylor's service record that he was on '8 days annual leave' from 29th July till the 5th August and that the others who had been at Upper Heyford were posted to the Heavy Conversion Unit on the 5th August, so it can safely be assumed that they also had the same spell of leave. The crew would now need a flight engineer versed in the mechanical requirements of the Lancaster Bomber. This was to be Sergeant Albert Rooks who had already joined the unit on the 24th July. Ewan spent five days from the 5th to the 9th August at Swinderby, the Group Base Station, before transferring to Wigsley, where he joined the rest of his crew. They were to be there for the best part of three months.

H.C.U. 1654 Wigsley (Nottinghamshire), seven miles to the West of the City of Lincoln, was situated between the villages of Wigsley and Spalford. The main runway crossed the Wigsley road and the airfield layout also included part of Wigsley Wood. Conditions were described as 'primitive'; in fact, one airman I spoke to, went so far as to call Wigsley a "dump". Bert Cole was a little more polite about it, describing the living conditions as 'very basic' and the food, 'poor'. Accommodation was in wooden huts. It was opened on the 8th February 1942 as a satellite for Swinderby and used at first by 455 RAAF Squadron operating with Hampdens. They moved out in April and the following month Wigsley became H.C.U. 1654 training crews in Manchesters and Lancasters to become fully operational for the squadrons of No.5 Group.

Bert Cole's pilot, Sgt Lou Watson, was instructed by Peter Langdon, eventually a Squadron Leader but then a twenty-year-old Sergeant Pilot Instructor, who was posted to Wigsley from the 10th April 1943 to the 3rd August that year. 'I arrived there straight from a short spell in hospital after I'd been driven into the rear end of a Lancaster at night by a young WAAF driver'. He could remember the pillars down the dining room of the Sergeants' Mess and that at the end there was a screened off secluded section for ground crew senior NCOs and instructors. 'I went there for my first meal at that mess. One of the staff told me that students ate at the other end of the room, and then he asked me why I wasn't moving there. He wanted to throw me out because I couldn't possibly be old enough to be an instructor'.

By 1943, Bomber Command was rapidly expanding. Most aircrew were wartime volunteers, there to replace the dwindling numbers of RAF regulars and the War was old enough now for even youngsters like Peter to have served time on operations in a squadron and gone on to instruct the up and coming in training units such as Wigsley.

When Peter was posted there in April there were insufficient Lancasters available and the older Manchesters were still in use. The twin engine Manchester, was the precursor of the four-engine Lancaster, but apart from this obvious difference, the two aircraft were very similar in design. The Manchester had been in service with the RAF from 1941 but had never been very successful, largely because it was underpowered, the two engines being insufficient to drive an aircraft with the frame of a heavy bomber. It was withdrawn from operations the following year but continued as a training aircraft till 1943. They were withdrawn from Wigsley in July of that year, so that by the time Ewan and his crew arrived all the aircraft were Lancasters. During his time there, he flew in either Lancaster Mark Is or Mark IIIs. The two types were almost identical in every aspect except that the Mark Is had British-built Rolls-Royce Merlin engines whereas the Mark IIIs had American-built Packard Merlins.

The Lancaster was the finest British bomber of World War II outclassing the Halifaxes and Stirlings in every aspect. It could also carry a heavier bomb load over a greater distance than the American B-17 Flying Fortress. The cockpit towered over nineteen feet above the ground with good all round vision and when a larger and improved forward blister was fitted in 1943, the bomb aimer had a better view than his counterpart in any other contemporary aircraft. In the cockpit the flight engineer sat beside the pilot. His main responsibility was to manage the engines and fuel for which there was a special panel of instruments but also to assist the pilot when necessary. He sat on a hinged seat that could be raised to allow the bomb aimer access to the nose. The latter would spend his time up to the target assisting the navigator with visual identification of features on the ground when visibility allowed. There was also a front gun turret he could man if needed.

Behind the cockpit the navigator sat sideways on, with his back to the main thoroughfare, curtained off to shield the light that shone on his table of charts and array of navigational instruments. Behind this was the wireless operator's compartment, its working table with Morse key, surrounded by radio equipment. He sat facing forwards with his back against the main spar, a waist-high barrier. He also had control of the heating for the aircraft. This was a particular drawback because the heating was not evenly distributed. If turned up to satisfy the requirements of the rest of the crew the wireless operator boiled. If he turned it down, the others froze.

Halfway down the fuselage between the rear edge of the wing and the tail was the mid-upper turret. The gunner accessed it by a step above the bomb bay and then clipped on a seat beneath him. The thoroughfare along the rear fuselage was packed with chains of ammunition for the guns and various other items of equipment including a rest bed and toilet. The loneliest station in the aircraft was the rear turret, so bitterly cold that "tail end Charlie" as he was affectionately called, was equipped with an electrically heated flying suit. By late 1943 gunners were beginning to remove some of the Perspex from their rear turrets to improve visibility, which would have exposed them still further to the icy conditions of 20,000 feet.

Such was the aircraft that my cousin Tom and his friends were to be trained in when they arrived at Wigsley on Thursday 5th August. Ewan didn't get there till the 9th, after his few days at Swinderby, but taking the length of time from 5th August till they were killed, on what the Operations Record Book describes as 'their final exercise' on the 22nd October, their posting at Wigsley lasted 79 days.

The two ORBs for Wigsley appear well organised, each with its own limitations. The briefer of the two describes the weather conditions, and the number of day and night flying hours, but is more expansive in listing the movements of commissioned officers in and out of the unit. The other is more detailed on a day-to-day basis, describing the type of exercise done and the daily position of the three courses that ran concurrently, together with the various entertainments laid on. Neither name the crews involved or the actual aircraft they flew and since most of the aircrew were Sergeants, including many of the Pilots, the ORB listing movements of commissioned officers is only of limited help. Also, notwithstanding the eternal problem of weather conditions that could hold up flying schedules, it will be seen that the apparent organisation of the training programme was very far from reality.

According to the ORB, courses lasted 36 days. Bert Cole was there that year from 21st March to 27th April: 38 days. When Ewan returned from Swinderby, Course 20 was starting, but this finished on 13th September. In fact, his crew were there long enough to have attended two courses consecutively. For this, their second course would have been No. 23, which finished on the 19th October, three days before they were killed. There was no reason for extending the course due to weather conditions because the weather had been good enough for extensive night flying from the 16th October right up to the day before they died. The most advanced course on the 22nd October was Day 27 of Course 24. If they were on this course it seems unlikely that the 'final exercise' was taking place with a further nine days to run?

Unfortunately, without their log books, we can't be certain what they were doing each day, so for this we have to turn to aircrew who survived. Jim Logan and Bill Pearson, both RCAF, and both Flying Officers by the end of the War, were, respectively, the navigator and bomb aimer in the crew of Sgt Johnny Kirkup RAF. They were at Wigsley from 9th August till 16th October: 69 days, almost the same time as Ewan and crew. They also were there almost long enough to attend two courses concurrently. Jim has no idea of what course they were on but his logbook records each flight they made. Their arrival at Wigsley coincided with the start of Course 20. On the 19th August this course was undergoing ground instruction, but Kirkup's crew were amongst four who carried out circuits and landings, which was supposed to be Day 21 of Course 19.

On the 1st October they were amongst six crews who did a searchlight and fighter cooperation exercise, which the ORB indicates as Day 28 of Course 22: a course that ended on the 9th October. But, their final flight was on the 16th October when they were amongst five crews who took part in a searchlight and fighter cooperation exercise, four of whom also completed a long cross-country. This was supposed to be Day 33 of Course 23, a course, according to the ORB, that contained another three days' flying instruction, but by the 19th, Kirkup's crew had already left Wigsley.

Obviously, in their case, they were not following any 36-day course as specifically numbered and as their time at the unit was almost the same as that of Taylor, it's fair to assume the same for him. End of month reports in the Wigsley ORBs are inconsistent in details given when dealing with postings. The report at the end of August only records the commissioned officers posted out. It's therefore impossible to trace whether other crews who started in August spent as much time in the unit as those of Taylor and Kirkup. Reports at the end of September and October are more detailed, particularly September. Of twenty-nine officers posted to Wigsley that month, ten who started Course 22 on the 4th and seven who started Course 23 on the 14th, were posted out during following month. As these courses were due to finish on the 9th and 19th

October respectively, it looks as if seventeen out of the twenty-nine followed the official thirty-six day course.

In the case of Johnny Kirkup and crew, an examination of Bill Pearson's log book shows that after a consistent programme of flights from the 15th August to the 8th September there was then a gap of 22 days till they resumed on the 1st October. This could in part be explained by a contagious infection amongst the Sergeants that put them in quarantine for a week or more, which Bill recalls occurred sometime during their stay at Wigsley. There were also over this period a few days when the weather was unsuitable and, of course, there might have been a few days leave, but it seems unlikely that this could have been the sole reason for a total lack of flying that accounted for over three weeks. The same epidemic could also have affected Ewan's crew, five of whom were Sergeants, and we know from his service record that he was on leave twice during his HCU Training amounting to 13 days, but again, there must have been other reasons for such an extended length of time at a Conversion Unit.

This inevitably raises the question why some aircrew spent much longer in training than others and some of the answer certainly lies in the problem of supply and demand. By 1943 the O.T.Us. and H.C.Us. were the final part of a lengthy production line from the initial recruitment stage to the fully trained crew. Demands required to man the number of operational aircraft determined the number of aircrew needed for the bomber squadrons at any one time.

Fluctuation of supply and demand can be seen from monthly reports concerning H.C.Us. made by Air Vice Marshal Capel, who was in command of the bomber crew training programme at the time. In a report for August 1943, dated 15th September, he wrote: 'It will be noted that at certain Conversion Units the number of hours per crew has extended very much beyond the normal course limits, and this is no doubt due to the fact that for a short period the production of crews in certain Groups is outrunning the vacancies in Squadrons. The Command has, however, been told to overproduce crews in the autumn against large expansion in the last quarter of the year, and no Group should give extended courses until they have at least fulfilled the full four-weekly output quota.' A month later he adds: 'It is again pointed out that it is essential that only crews who definitely require further training above the normal Course should be given this extra flying, and this will obviously apply to only a few below average crews whose extra flying cannot raise the average flying per crew by any large figure. All above average and average crews should require only the planned Course.' That same month he commented on the shortage of Lancasters in No.5 Group, to which Wigsley belonged. In his report for October he lamented the bad weather that caused a loss of 107 crews in estimated output, but added: 'The only bright spot is No.5 Group who achieved more than the estimated output', but: 'with flying hours per crew slightly below normal'.

This could, at least in part, explain what was happening at Wigsley. Commanding Officers were being urged to push as many crews through the system as possible but this was dependant on the number of aircraft available for training, of which there was a shortage of Lancasters. It was reckoned that any one aircraft should average 40 flying hours per month. The number of serviceable aircraft at Wigsley remained fairly constant from August to October (25, 26 & 24 respectively) but if a larger number of crews were coming up from the OTUs it would create a bottleneck with insufficient aircraft for all to fly. At the same time, COs were being urged not to extend flying hours except for crews who needed it and to keep the average down as far as possible. It seems likely that the completion of some crews' training, like those of Johnny and Ewan, were put on hold whilst the new intake was given some flying time. The overproduction of crews required in the autumn was probably anticipating the coming campaign to bomb Berlin, which during the end of 1943 and start of 1944 cost Bomber Command so many lives. Of the twenty-nine officers posted out of Wigsley that October, sixteen were to lose their lives, all within the next nine months.

During the course of that month the unit produced thirty-five pilots with average flying hours of 21 by day and 17.5 by night. Johnny Kirkup's were very similar: just over 23 by day and just under 17 by night. Ewan Taylor, according to the official Accident Report, flew a total of 22 hours, 9 of which were at night and his last flight was his 'final exercise'. In other words, his total day flying at Wigsley amounted to 13 hours and night flying would probably have been about 11 had he returned safely. We know from a deleted entry in the service record of Eric Williams that they would have been posted to 467 Squadron had they not been killed. This was an Australian squadron who'd lost a Lancaster on a raid to Hanover three days earlier. The choice of squadron was probably due to Ewan being RAAF.

Squadrons in Bomber Command were divided into Groups each served by three H.C.Us. The three units were scheduled to supply their Group with 104 crews every four weeks. As Capel pointed out, this amounted to '108 less 4% wastage'. In other words, it was expected that four or five crews per month in any three HCUs would for one reason or another fail to complete the conversion process. Taylor and crew were part of this grim statistic. Already in 1943, Wigsley had had its share of crashed aircraft on training exercises, both Manchesters and Lancasters. Of the Manchesters, one had crashed on 26th January and another as it approached the airfield on 15th April. The Manchesters were soon phased out but the Lancasters fared no better. By the end of May that year there had already been three major accidents. On the 11th June, Sgt William Featherstone in Lancaster ED833 was returning over Lincoln from a 'short cross country' when he crashed at 5.22 p.m., 'for reasons unknown', into a residential area of the city suburbs demolishing two houses in Highfield Avenue off the Skellingthorpe Road. Several of the local residents were killed and all the crew, except for the rear gunner who was injured and taken to hospital. Even a burst tyre could be potentially fatal. It happened to ED591 when taking off for an exercise on the night of 26th July. The Lancaster 'swung to starboard, colliding with some small trees' (ORB). The aircraft was a write-off but this time the crew were lucky and escaped unhurt.

The loss of a valuable plane through a burst tyre was bad enough but far worse was to come on two successive nights a month later. On 30th August, W4260 collided with a Halifax on the outskirts of Lincoln. Both pilots managed to crash-land, the Lancaster at Skellingthorpe whilst the Halifax struggled on to Ossington. By a miracle, both crews survived uninjured, though the Lancaster was a write-off. The normal outcome of such collisions, however, was fatal and so it was to prove the following night. Sgt MacDonald in R5698 and three other Lancasters had taken off on a long cross country involving 'searchlight and fighter co-operation' together with 'photo flash bombing and a dummy mining run'. Also on board was F/O Bernard Jobling, a staff navigation officer who had been posted to Wigsley from 157 Squadron. They had completed their exercise and were in the Southwell area not far from base, when they collided with JB132, a Lancaster out of Syerston. The latter crashed in flames near Bleasby. Jobling, MacDonald and all his crew were killed. Just over a fortnight later, on the 17th September, the ORB reported that Lancaster W4921 'swung on take off for exercise 21, (03 runway) struck BATTLE HEADQUARTERS and crashed in flames against rifle range.' But, in this case: 'crew escaped'.

The margin between life and death could depend on a whim. On 27th March that year, Sgt Lou Watson had been out with his crew in Manchester L7280 practising "circuits and bumps". Only the pilot and wireless operator were actively involved, the rest of the crew, essentially passengers. Sgt Bert Cole, the bomb aimer, was getting pretty fed up with the endless routine and wanted to finish for the day. When Watson mentioned another half hour's practice, Bert suggested that they put it to the vote. Three wanted to continue, three wanted to stop. Sgt Maurice Scarfe, the rear gunner, one of the Americans who had joined the RCAF whilst the USA were still neutral, was undecided. Bert tempted him with a free egg and chips at the Bridge Hotel, Saxilby, if he voted with them. Such a bribe was impossible for Maurice to resist and after some little time the truck arrived to take them back. They all piled in and had started to pull away when Lou looked back, and to his horror, saw the Manchester's port engine on fire.

The exhaust manifold had burnt through. As Bert said: 'Scarfe's egg and chips saved our bacon.'

Such 'familiarization flights including circuits and landings', according to his logbook, occupied navigator Jim Logan and his pilot, Johnny Kirkup, for three days in August. Despite the façade of 'Courses' and 'Days' entered in the ORB, presumably, to satisfy Headquarters, there was a methodical pattern of training at Wigsley and a good effort put in to get the crews up whenever possible. In fact, from August to October that year, according to the records, 'Actual Flying Hours' exceeded 'Expected Flying Hours' despite the weather. From the logbook of Bill Pearson, bomb aimer in Johnny Kirkup's crew, the conversion process can be clearly seen, starting with daylight flying: 15th Aug. familiarization flight with an instructor, 17th Aug. familiarization flight with instructor, circuit and landing with Johnny Kirkup, 'check circuit' with instructor, 19th Aug. 'check circuit' with instructor, local flying with Johnny, 23rd Aug. 3-engined landings with instructor, 24th Aug. 'cross country bombing – firing' with Johnny, then their first night flying: 'night familiarization' with instructor, 25th Aug. (night) circuits and landings, cross country bombing, both with Johnny, 26th Aug. (day) 'combat manoeuvre' with instructor, 30th Aug. (day) cross country bombing with Johnny, 3rd Sep. (day) 'fighter affiliation' with instructor, 8th Sep. (day) fighter affiliation with Johnny, (then the long gap of 22 days), 1st – 16th Oct. nine more flights, some by day and some by night, including searchlight affiliation and a final night cross country.

Ewan Taylor and crew would have been involved in a similar, though abridged version of this training programme. We also know from the Accident Report that he spent four hours in a Link Trainer. Harry Yates (*'Luck and a Lancaster'*) encountered this device for the first time whilst training in Tiger Moths and has a very graphic description of the experience: 'To look at, it was just a box with wings. The victim, for that was what it felt like, climbed into the box and a hood was closed over his head. Darkness reigned, save for the luminous glow of the instrument panel.' Harry found it 'far more difficult and sensitive to control than an aeroplane. It was a real pig to fly, added to which was the claustrophobia and, in August, the heat of the cockpit. When the lesson was finally over and the hood thrown back I, for one, always scrambled out drenched in sweat and feeling a hopeless failure.'

The general practice in Fighter Affiliation, when at night, ('*Night Fighter*', *Rawnsley & Wright*) was for the night fighter to signal when it had made an attack by flashing its navigation lights on and off. 'The bomber indicated that it had fired at a night fighter by flashing a torch from the gunner's turret. Time and again on these exercises we found that we could make our usual stalk and pull up and hold the bomber in the gun sight and sit there for several minutes before there was any response. Sometimes we could even finish the attack and pull up alongside the bomber, flashing our lights.' It was extremely difficult for the inexperienced to detect the stealthy approach of a radar equipped fighter but with practice 'a fully operational Lancaster taking full cork-screw evasion called for a great deal of chasing, and that was without the tail and mid-upper gunners pumping lead at us'.

Evading fighter attacks, termed in the ORB, 'operational defence manoeuvres', or in Bill's log book, 'combat manoeuvres', time and distance runs, GEE navigation and practice bombing were incorporated into long cross country exercises, and there was air to sea firing practice for the gunners. There were classes on ditching drill, dinghies and air/sea rescue. There were general lectures, like Crew Co-Operation, and specialist lectures on navigation and morse practice. Then, eventually, came the day for a crew's final exercise, sometimes called a 'Command Bullseye'. Such occurred on 25th September, when the ORB records: '5 crews took part in a "COMMAND BULLSEYE", their final cross-country, which included searchlight and fighter co-operation over most of the route, a time and distance run and Infra Red bombing on various targets. The "COMMAND BULLSEYE" was of 5 hours duration approximately.'

After four nights when flying was cancelled due to bad weather, Johnny Kirkup's crew took part in their final exercise on 16th October and with ten other crews completed what the ORB more modestly termed 'a long cross-country which included practice bombing'. Jim Logan's logbook describes it as a 'searchlight affiliation & cross country' lasting four hours forty minutes. It covered a lengthy route ranging from the South Midlands to the Scottish Border and return via the North Sea: 'Base – Kings Lynn – March – Kettering – Bedford – Cambridge – March – Lincoln – Jedburgh – 5600N.0200E – 5333N.0200E – Holkham – Kings Lynn – Base.' This is the type of route Ewan and his crew in L7575 would have taken six days later when after flying for an hour and a quarter they were near St Albans. The five crews that night would have probably followed the same route but with take-offs staggered to avoid collision. For the four crews that returned safely it must have been a difficult and disappointing final exercise. The weather was so poor that fighter affiliation and Infra Red bombing had to be cancelled. Only searchlight co-operation was possible.

Like fighter affiliation, searchlight co-operation required the assistance of our anti-aircraft defences to give the trainee crews some vital practice before they encountered the real thing. Jim Logan describes such an exercise, which lasted three and a half hours. Their route was: 'Base – Gainsboro – Malton – Market Rasen – Tuxford. It appears that we may have gone around all or part of this route twice'. Anti-aircraft batteries would have been alerted that friendly aircraft were taking part, to focus their lights, not their guns, and as for bombing practice, Ewan would have taken his crew to Wainfleet Sands, on the Lincolnshire Coast, where eleven and a half pound bombs were dropped: smoke by day or flash by night.

John Thwaite arrived at Wigsley on the last day of August. For reasons unknown Ewan's original bomb aimer was not amongst the crew who plunged to their deaths on the 22nd October. Sometime during those last seven weeks John replaced him. He would have had to get used to the new crew he was working with, especially the navigator, Eric Williams, who, no doubt, was continuing to practise with the 'Gee-box' on cross-country flights. We know from John's obituary that the crew flew over his home in the Lake District on one such exercise just a few nights before their final flight. Meanwhile,

Ewan Taylor and Albert Rooks, his flight engineer, would have been learning to work together at the cockpit controls. Albert was already familiar with the Lancaster from his time at St Athan and visit to the Avro Works.

Norman Ashton, another flight engineer, paints a confident picture of his training at an H.C.U. in his book, 'Only Birds and Fools'. 'I soon accustomed myself to moving the correct levers and pushing the correct buttons. He mentions 'two- and three-engined flying, flapless landings, overshoots and stalls', in which Ewan and Albert would have been involved. 'The final exercise was a Bullseye and this was carried out in true operational style. We had a pukka briefing and were instructed to treat the whole thing with the seriousness of an actual operational mission. We had a trouble-free trip and confirmed the confidence we felt in ourselves, in each other, and in the type of aircraft we were to fly.'

Much depended on the particular aircraft available at the time and the quality of instruction. Harry Yates ('*Luck and a Lancaster*') describes the downside of the training programme, in which he writes that many of the aircraft at the operational training units 'were patently clapped out and, often, poorly maintained'. As for the instructors, he writes: 'most of them were selected from tour-expired aircrew. Almost all were decorated. After the intensity and comradeship of life on a front-line squadron, instruction must have seemed like a world of shadows to them. Finding their work boring and without satisfaction, I think many merely went through the motions'.

But, probably for most, the truth lay somewhere between these points of view, and though training units might have been safer for the instruction staff than when they were in the front line, it was still quite possible for them to get killed. Wing Commander Charles Stenning DSO DFC was a veteran of over sixty sorties in the earlier part of the War. He had taken up pilots like Guy Gibson and John Hopgood on familiarization flights when Lancasters had first been supplied to the squadrons the previous year. He was Chief Flying Instructor at Wigsley from January to August 1943, but was posted elsewhere a few days after Ewan's crew arrived. His son remembers him talking about training pilots: 'Father always said it could be quite a test of nerves with some, as there was very little you could do if one made a serious error while flying.' Charles Stenning survived the War but many didn't. Instructors like Bernard Jobling were amongst approximately 1,500 aircrew lost in training accidents during 1943.

11. Time Off

It's already been noted how some of those who were trained overseas spent quite a long time at Personnel Reception Centres before being posted elsewhere. These periods of delay in the training process seemed to vary from one individual to another. For young men who had been put through intensive courses of training it was an opportunity to relax and socialise; a welcome break in comparative safety before the inevitable uncertainty and danger that lay ahead. 'There was a very apt expression in vogue in those days', writes Ross Blanchard, friend of Bruce Davies. 'That was: "Hurry up and wait"!' After arriving in England in early July '43, he spent over two months at the PRC in Brighton and by a chance encounter managed to put his musical talents to good use.

>   'Very shortly after arriving, my best mate Angus Tyson, a very good pianist in the "Fats Waller" style and I were walking along the seafront when we saw a sign that said "OUT OF BOUNDS TO ALL SERVICE PERSONNEL". Now, being Aussies our mental telepathy message said, if it's out of bounds it must be interesting. Without a word to each other we went down a flight of stairs and into a very large room with a full length bar, complete with barman, about forty tables with several very comfortable chairs to each one, a good carpeted floor apart from the dance floor, a podium with a semi-grand piano and a full kit of drums complete with sticks and brushes. The three of us were the only people in the room for it was the one day of the week that it was not open. After a while one of us asked the barman if he would mind if we played a bit of music and he was only too pleased to say "yes". We had a ball and after about an hour of this top quality jazz, the barman asked us if we would be interested in playing six nights a week for ten shillings each a night, plus all we

could drink for free. Now, there's no way any logical person would refuse such an offer and we started the next night.'

'It became very popular, was overcrowded every evening and the group grew from a duet to a nine-piece band. After about a month my good mate was posted to do some more training but it did not take long to get another pianist. Shortly after this, a man came up to us during our evening break and introduced himself as the Manager of "The Dome" dance hall and asked if we would be interested in giving their band a fifteen minute break every hour for ten shillings each plus free drinks at the bar. Once again, there was no way we could say "no" and if you put a wholesale price on our freebies plus five guineas tax free pay a week, we were each earning more than the Air Force paid us. They were great days.'

In 1943, a pint of beer at your local would have cost you 7d (*3p*) and the average factory worker was earning £5/13/9d (*£5.70p*) per week. The need for extra production had boosted jobs and pay. Aircrew wages seem poor by comparison, considering the risks involved. Even those of similar rank could be on a completely different scale of remuneration. It all depended on the degree of training involved. For example, the weekly earnings of an aircrew sergeant would amount to £4/14/6d (*£4.73p*) if he was a pilot, navigator or bomb aimer, £4/4/0d (*£4.20p*) for a flight engineer or wireless operator, but only £2/16/0d (*£2.80p*) for an air gunner. The idea was that, for instance, it would take eighteen months to train a navigator to achieve the same degree of competence in his crew position that an air gunner could attain in ten weeks. Nor did the danger factor apply, because a ground crew engine fitter of equivalent rank earned £3/13/6d (*£3.68p*).

One of the ground crew at Wigsley was Allan Walter Jones (*see photograph*), from Bristol, who had joined the RAF on 26th May 1937. After various postings he had arrived at Wigsley on the 13th June 1942 where he was to spend the rest of his War service except for a short spell of training at Coningsby in the spring of 1943. By now a corporal and fully experienced fitter with a thorough working knowledge of Merlin engines, he had originally hoped to volunteer for aircrew and train as a flight engineer. Unfortunately, this was not to be. Part of his previous experience had been at sea aboard the aircraft carrier HMS *Furious* with No.13 MU (*Maintenance Unit*) on a voyage from Greenock to West Africa. On board ship, much of his work was spent in a hangar below decks where his unit assembled and tested Hurricanes prior to them being flown off to Takoradi. Without ear protection, the incessant racket of the Merlins in a confined space had perforated his eardrums and rendered him medically unfit to fly.

On an airbase, and particularly at training units, there was a distinct social division between aircrew who were just passing through and permanent staff like the ground crews who maintained the aircraft. When off duty, each went their separate ways. The Station Hotel in the nearby village of Saxilby was the haunt of Allan and his mates. There, the landlady used to make them feel at home: so much so, that eventually Allan married her daughter, Lorna, settled there after the War, and had a family, some of whom still live in the village.

As for aircrew, once airborne, the pilot gave the orders even if he was lower in rank than others in the crew. Also, when off the base, crews would fraternise on equal terms whatever their rank or background but social differences were maintained on the bases with commissioned officers and sergeants each having a separate mess. In the case of Johnny Kirkup and his crew, training was held up for a week or more when a contagious infection was discovered amongst NCOs on the base and they had to be quarantined. Bill Pearson RCAF, then a Pilot Officer, relates how Johnny and the other sergeants 'in our crew were billeted in a hut distanced from main mess hall sections. They were brought food etc from mess hall but were contained in the hut. There was a big Officers Mess party one afternoon and the beer was flowing freely. Later in the evening another buddy and I thought it was a shame that the rest of our crews couldn't enjoy it. I remember us struggling to roll a small barrel of beer from behind the mess tent and through a short cut to the quarantined via a potato field. It was deposited at the door of their hut and the rest was up to them. A lot was spilled in their attempts to open the keg but they succeeded somehow and all had some beer. The delivery guys disappeared post haste and were never reprimanded.'

Amongst the training staff at Wigsley, Peter Langdon, the young Sergeant Instructor, who was twenty-one on the 10th July 1943, recalls: 'the nearest town was Lincoln and there was a regular bus service, but the town was flooded out with RAF personnel and there was a semi-permanent shortage of beer in the town and possibly not enough girls to go round. A number of us used to go to a pub at Dunholme Bridge and we travelled there by bicycle.' It was run by an ex-RAF man and his wife who extended their hospitality towards airmen by continuing to serve them after closing time. Peter recalls that on one occasion it was past midnight when they were disturbed by a knock on the door and in marched a constable from the local police force. However, instead of serving the licensee with a summons, he ordered a pint and sat down with them.

If Peter had gone to Lincoln, he could have seen a play at the Theatre Royal, or gone to the cinema at the Central or the Regal, which had its own café. Or he might have preferred an evening drinking at the Saracen's Head Hotel or the Stonebow, known to aircrew as the 'Snakepit'. But, if there was a shortage of girls at Lincoln, rumour had it that there was an over abundance at Nottingham and that they were the prettiest in England. Ewan's crew had arrived at Wigsley during the August Bank Holiday week at the height of the Goose Fair. The girls would have been out in the parks or at the fun fair in their summer dresses and the "boys in blue" were always popular. In fact, it wasn't unknown for aircrew to walk into a pub and have a pint in their hands before they'd even had a chance to order.

Nottingham was undoubtedly one of the favourite haunts of airmen from Wigsley and surrounding bases and there was the usual variety of entertainment on hand. Like Lincoln, there was a Theatre Royal. There was the Astoria cinema or pubs like the White Hart and the Flying Horse, both favourites of Johnny Kirkup and his crew. Opposite the Flying Horse there was the Black Boy or some airmen preferred the Trip to Jerusalem. But, if they fancied something more energetic, there was the Palais de Danse, conveniently situated next to the bus station.

The Canadian Jim Logan recalls: 'going with Johnny Kirkup and some of the crew to the Palais de Danse in Nottingham and meeting a girl there from Lound who worked in a war industry in Nottingham. We enjoyed dancing and I continued to take her out when I had time off from 9 Squadron in Bardney. She invited me to her home in Lound one weekend and I met her parents and younger sister. Her father was a sergeant in the Home Guard.' Jim's experience was pretty typical of aircrew from overseas, who contributed so much to the war effort, many with their lives. They were made welcome in Britain. Ewan and Bruce would have had similar opportunities and it's possible that there was romance in Ewan's life if an apocryphal story of his untimely death can be believed.

Not only were there opportunities that summer for aircrew personnel to meet up with girls in the local towns but there were also W.A.A.Fs. on the bases. In fact, the establishment at Wigsley in that summer and autumn of 1943 made some considerable effort to entertain the young men and women there if the operations record book is anything to go by. On the 5th August, the day Ewan's crew arrived, 'An enjoyable cycle run to South Clifton and swimming in the Trent was held'. Then that evening: 'A Concert was given by the Fiskerton Concert Party to a full house'. On the 7th August: 'A cricket match between the Station and R.A.F. Waddington resulted in a win for Waddington by 67 – 41 runs. A tennis match was also played between a Station team and R.A.F. Waddington'. On the 17th August: 'A Dance for all ranks was held in the Station Cinema. The R.A.F. Regiment Band provided the Music and light refreshments also helped to make the evening a pleasant one'.

Two days later, at 8 p.m., it was the turn of the W.A.A.Fs. to hold a social in their N.A.A.F.I. 'Music for dancing was provided by the Station Band, light refreshments were provided by the N.A.A.F.I. and a few games of table tennis were played'. Previously, at 6.30, there had been a meeting in the station cinema 'for all personnel interested in football'. With the onset of autumn, on the 2nd October: 'A football match was played between the Station Team and H.Q.48 Division, Home Forces, commencing at 14.30 hours on the Station Ground'. The result is not recorded.

An attempt was made to cater for all tastes. There were films produced by E.N.S.A. (*the Entertainments National Service Association*) held in the station cinema such as 'Two Yanks in Trinidad' (22nd August), or on 30th September audiences were offered George Bernard Shaw's play, 'Man and Superman'. Quality could vary, such as two nights previously, when the ORB records: 'An ENSA show took place in the Station Cinema. This was rather a poor show, but provided some entertainment to a full house'. Such productions earned ENSA the unfair acronym "Every Night Something Awful", because, certainly, this was not the case.

Apart from ENSA productions there were plenty of other films shown in the station cinema. Some came from the Canadian Salvation Army Unit, designed to illustrate the war effort, such as 'Coastal Command' (8th Oct). Audiences were even given the opportunity to see the depths of Nazi propaganda on the 25th September when the 'Pied Piper' was shown to a 'full house'. For the more musically inclined, the station cinema was the venue on the 6th October for a 'classical' concert, given by the R.A.F. Central Orchestra, but, such visits were obviously rare. Most of the time the best that could be offered were 'Classical Gramophone Recitals' such as the one in the W.A.A.F. N.A.A.F.I. on the 17th October.

Those preferring more active participation could opt for a 'Whist Drive', such as on the 13th October, when 'prizes were awarded and a pleasant evening was enjoyed by a large crowd'. The night before they could have even played Bingo, or 'Housey Housey' as it was then known. And, if you hadn't learned how to dance there was plenty of opportunity at Wigsley. On 4th October: 'Dancing classes were held in the Station Cinema, followed by one hours dancing to Gramophone Records'.

Thus, there was plenty of opportunity for Ewan and his friends to participate in the social life at the base. From the testimony of their families, it is known that Thwaite, Rooks and Davies had girlfriends back home, which in the case of Bruce's sweetheart, Carlien, was on the other side of the world. Both he and Ewan, had received further promotion during their final spell of training at Wigsley, Ewan to Pilot Officer on the 24th August and Bruce to Flight Sergeant on the 4th September. In their distinctive dark blue RAAF uniforms they could always find a welcome at Australia House in the Strand where they could meet up and have a drink with their mates downstairs in the Boomerang Club. We know that Bruce visited London at least once when he met up with his old friend Ross Blanchard. Ross had family friends, Mr and Mrs Holiday, who owned a flat in Grosvenor Square where they stayed for a day or two that summer.

Bruce had plenty of relatives in the U.K. and he must have taken heed of his grandfather and gone to visit them during his spells of leave. On the 4th August, the last day of his week's leave before being posted to Wigsley, he was visiting his father's cousin, John Wilson, the musician and teacher at Charterhouse School, Farncombe, Surrey, to whom his grandfather had written earlier that year. The weather was fine and dry. That morning, in the town of Godalming, close by, a little three-year-old boy (*myself*) was out with his father at the allotments digging vegetables and in the afternoon with his mother in the park. Meanwhile, Bruce had been playing cricket with John Wilson's two young sons, Christopher and Anthony, in the garden of their house near the school. There's a delightful photo to mark the event. With a splendid plane tree in full leaf as a background, Bruce is sitting on the garden roller and either side of him are the two boys, Christopher clutching a cricket ball and little Anthony, not much bigger than the bat he's holding.

Just down the hill, in Farncombe, my cousin, Tom, was spending the week's leave with his parents. They had been fortunate in escaping from their house in London when it was destroyed in the Blitz and had found lodgings in the comparative safety of the Surrey countryside. There's a photograph of him with his mother in the tiny back garden of their temporary home. Short in stature, he stands there, smiling in his sergeant's stripes, dwarfing the proud little woman at his side. These were the last known photos taken of Tom and Bruce. It is entirely conceivable that Bruce might have paid Tom a visit at Farncombe and that they might have travelled up to Wigsley together the following day.

Unlike Tom's father, who had retired, Eddie's father was still in the Metropolitan Police and the young air gunner would have returned home on leave to their house in Glebe Road, just a stone's throw from Hornsey Railway Station. Eric's parents were also close to the rail network in Station Road, Manor Park. Though now in his early thirties he was single and Manor Park, North London was still his home. The other older member of the crew, Ewan, was also single. When he emigrated to Australia a few years before, he had left many relatives in the U.K., foremost of whom was his father, in Clifton, Bristol, so, there must have been a number of homes to welcome him.

According to his service record, he was on leave for four days from the 24th to the 27th September. It would seem that the rest of his crew were in the same position, for my father wrote in his diary for Sunday the 26th September that Tom had visited our home that evening: 'He has 4 day's leave. He stayed to supper & went at 9.30. He had very interesting things to say.' Such information, whatever it was, would have certainly concerned his activities in the RAF and might well have been of a confidential nature.

Tom walked out of our lives that evening. We were never to see him again, for when news came through that he was reported 'missing', my father noted in his diary that this had been the last time we saw him. However, Ewan had his last spell of leave from the 5th to the 13th October and it seems almost certain that the others were on leave at the same time. Bill, John Thwaite's brother, who was then a staff sergeant in the R.E.M.E., was stationed at Melton Mowbray. He had an army car and drove to Nottingham one day where he met John who had travelled there by rail. They had lunch and spent the rest of the day together. Normally very open with one another, Bill detected a certain reserve and unease in John's manner. The exact reason for this, he can't be sure. Perhaps John was viewing with some apprehension the prospect of facing the danger ahead with a crew he had only just joined. He was certainly very aware of the high casualty rate. Bill reckons, though he can't be definite, that this meeting took place about ten days before his brother was killed which would put it towards the end of Ewan's leave.

Mabel, Albert Rooks' young sister, remembers her brother's last spell of leave in Leeds: 'he always used to bring home his dirty washing and my mother would do it for him, as there were no facilities at the base.'

Albert had a girlfriend and they were serious; so much so, that they planned to be engaged. But, there was a problem because the girl had a former boyfriend serving overseas and she wanted to break the news to him personally when he returned to the U.K. before she made her engagement to Albert official. He was extremely shy about having his photograph taken but she persuaded him at the last moment and so we have a good picture of him in his sergeant's stripes and flight engineer brevet. However, by the time the film had been developed Albert was dead and, as can be imagined, it was heartrending for his mother to see that photo for the first time. Mabel reckons that he was last with them only a short while before he was killed and the fact that the photo was still at the photographers would tend to support this.

With his last spell of leave at an end, amongst tearful farewells, Albert confessed to his mother that he didn't want to go back. Mabel still thinks that he somehow knew he wouldn't see them again, and so it was to prove, for a few days later he was lying dead in the orchard of a Hertfordshire farm.

12. The Aircraft

L7575 was a Mark 1 Lancaster powered by four Rolls Royce Merlin XX engines. After the three prototypes, it was in the first batch of forty-three Lancasters (*L7527-L7549 & L7565-L7584*) ever to be built. A.V. Roe & Co. of Newton Heath, Manchester, had originally been under contract to build 200 Manchesters (the twin-engine precursors of the Lancaster) but the order was amended to 157 Manchesters and 43 Lancasters. These Lancasters were delivered to the RAF between October 1941 and March 1942. 44 Squadron was the first to fly operational sorties with the Lancaster Bomber in early March, followed by 97 Squadron later that month.

Commencing January 1942, 97 Squadron received nine of the first batch. L7575 was sent to them on the 13th March just before their move from Coningsby to Woodhall Spa in Lincolnshire. It was to fly under the code letters 'OF-Y' on its fuselage. Operations, in which a few Lancasters from either squadron were involved, continued till the 26th March, by which time 97 Squadron had received a dozen more aircraft from the second batch sent out from the Avro works, bearing serial numbers prefixed with the letter 'R'.

So far, all had gone relatively smoothly but then, on the 26th, the squadron was ordered to withdraw all Lancasters from operations, as one had been lost due to structural failure of the outer wing. Headquarters of No.5 Group signalled:

> *'Lancaster A/C to be inspected immediately for failure of flush rivets attaching the wing tip skin to rib attachment to mainplane and wrinkling of skin on the top surface. Aircraft defective are to be grounded until further instructions. Aircraft not defective may be flown on practice flights only, with light load inboard tanks only. Remaining tanks to be empty.'*

Eight aircraft were withdrawn from 97 Squadron for repair and operations did not recommence until 8th April. It's not certain whether L7575 was amongst the faulty aircraft. There's no record in the Squadron's Operations Record Book of which aircraft were affected. What is certain is that it must have been declared fully operational soon after this date because it was about to embark on a brief but glorious career, lasting a week and consisting of two missions.

On the night of 10th/11th April, four Lancasters of 97 Squadron and four from 44 Squadron were detailed to be part of a force of 254 bombers in a raid on the Krupps Factory at Essen in the Ruhr Valley, or "Happy Valley" as it came to be ruefully called. One of the 97 Squadron aircraft didn't take off, due to engine trouble. Another bombed the alternative target, Cologne, but two found their way to Essen. One of these was L7575, skippered by Squadron Leader Dugdale, with his crew of Sergeant Croppi, Flight Sergeants Bennett and Turner, Pilot Officer Grieves and Sergeants Martin and Linnett. They took off at 2211 hours. On arrival the target was shrouded in 9/10ths cloud so they dropped their bombs from 18,500 feet on green flares. As the ground was invisible the bursts were not seen. They were not troubled by the 'occasional' heavy flak beneath them but noted that the searchlights were 'accurate'. However, L7575 brought them home unscathed at 0306 hours. This was the penultimate raid of eight that had been carried out against Essen over the past month but the results were not particularly encouraging with very little damage inflicted on the Krupps Factory.

A few days later L7575 took part in one of the most daring raids undertaken by Bomber Command during World War II. In the first half of April, 44 Squadron and 97 Squadron carried out a series of low level training flights and it became obvious that something special was being planned. On the 14th April they flew on a lengthy exercise ending in a simulated attack on Inverness and the rumour spread amongst the crews that they were going to attack a German warship. This however was very far from the truth, though there was, in fact, a naval connection. Sir Arthur Harris, C-in-C Bomber Command, now had at his command a new bomber with a capability far exceeding any other of its type. With this he intended to prove that he could attack targets previously beyond the normal range of his aircraft. The German submarine fleet were crippling our supply lines across the Atlantic and the Maschinenfabrik Augsburg-Nurnberg Aktiengesellschaft factory, known as the "M.A.N. Factory", at Augsburg, manufactured diesel engines for the U-Boats. Its location, in Southern Germany, involved a 1500-mile flight.

Nothing had prepared the crews for the shock that awaited them as they filed into the briefing rooms on the 17th April. The factory area was no larger than a football pitch, so it was decided to carry out the attack at low level in daylight. Each aircraft carried four 1000 lb bombs with delayed action fuses. Squadron Leader John Nettleton headed six Lancasters from 44 Squadron and Squadron Leader John Sherwood, the same number from 97 Squadron. The aircraft from each squadron were further subdivided into two sections of three.

Flying Officer Ernest Deverill was pilot of L7575, the second in the rear section of 97 Squadron. He had started as a pupil of No.1 School of Technical Training at RAF Halton, where:

> '...apprentices and boys were trained to become technical staff to service and repair aircraft. Deverill had outstanding natural ability, and overcoming all the usual conventions he had remustered as a pilot in 1938. He had flown over a hundred sorties, most of them for Coastal Command, before he once again bucked the norm and became an officer, having worked his way up from the very bottom of the ladder. There is no doubt that he was a superb pilot'[1]

By the time of the Augsburg operation he had already been awarded the DFM.

A plan was evolved for concealing the target's identity from the German defences for as long as possible by crossing the French coast and then changing direction twice before approaching Augsburg from the South. The two squadrons,

---

[1] From *Fire by Night* by Jennie Gray.

headed by Nettleton's six aircraft, were to fly two miles apart and the Luftwaffe fighters were to be kept busy fending off diversionary attacks by the RAF over Northern France.

L7575 took off at 1469 hours with Deverill and his crew of Sergeant Cooper, Pilot Officer Butler, Sergeants Irons, MacKay and Devine and Flight Sergeant Keane. Two extra Lancasters from the Squadron were scheduled as reserves but one of these was grounded with mechanical problems. The other flew as far as Selsey Bill, where the six aircraft from either squadron successfully rendezvoused, then, surplus to requirements, returned to base. Take-off time had been planned for around 3 p.m. so that the twelve Lancasters would reach the target by dusk and return under cover of darkness.

The diversionary raids had brought up the German fighters and, unchallenged, the two squadrons skimmed across the Channel at a height of fifty feet. Nettleton's six drew ahead of Sherwood's as planned. All went well until Nettleton drew too close to a fighter airfield just as a group of Messerschmitts and Focke-Wulfs were about to land after returning from an engagement with the RAF diversionary attacks to the North. Several spotted the rear of Nettleton's formation and gave chase. Within a few minutes all three Lancasters were shot down and the Germans went on to attack the leading section. They managed to shoot down one of these but after half an hour shortage of fuel obliged them to return to base. Nettleton and the other remaining aircraft in his section finally arrived at the target and pressed home their attack but the other aircraft had been hit on the run in and crashed just afterwards. As darkness closed in, Nettleton nursed his damaged aircraft back and was awarded the V.C. for his bravery.

As they approached the target, the six Lancasters of 97 Squadron, just two miles behind him, had not been spotted by the German fighters. They were flying so low that they had to pull up to avoid factory chimneys before diving back to roof top height. When they arrived the German defences were fully alerted and poured a hail of gunfire into the leading section. Sherwood's Lancaster hit the ground and exploded just after it had released its bombs, the other two survived. By the time the rear section attacked, the German gunners knew the exact angle of approach and their fire was deadlier than ever. One aircraft, already on fire, managed to complete its attack before it exploded.

L7575 was badly hit. Sergeant Ron Irons, its wireless operator, recounts in Peter Jacobs' book, 'The Lancaster Story': 'we were flying as number two of the rear section and by the time that we arrived over the target area the element of surprise had completely gone. The German defences were very alert and were firing everything imaginable at us, including heavy gunfire. We were hit during the run-in to the target. Flak had hit the hydraulic pipes, which had put the gun turrets out of action, and hydraulic oil had caught fire under the mid-upper turret. I left my position to help Sergeant MacKay, the mid-upper gunner, extinguish the fire.'

At the same time the port outer engine had been hit and was on fire. As L7575 pulled away from the target trailing flames, Deverill had a real problem on his hands. It was still light, visibility was good. MacKay and Irons were getting the fires in the starboard fuselage and bomb bay under control. The port engine had been feathered. With both turrets out of action the aircraft was defenceless. Bombing at low level, from 400 feet, they had no height but as night fell they must try to climb on the three remaining engines. Deverill, with great skill, managed to nurse L7575 up to 18,000 feet and before reaching the coast they'd even succeeded in restarting the stricken engine. They had also kept in touch with their formation leader, Flying Officer Penman DFC in Lancaster R5496 who afforded them some degree of protection.

They finally got back to Woodhall Spa at 2315 hours. Riddled with shell holes including a ten-foot gash along the fuselage, severely damaged from fire and with both turrets out of action, L7575 was immediately declared a write-off. Deverill was awarded the DFC to add to his DFM, whilst Irons and MacKay were each given the DFM for their prompt action to extinguish the fires, thus saving the aircraft from immediate destruction. Reports of the attack were highly publicised in the papers and on the radio. Messages of congratulations were received from the Air Chiefs and Prime Minister.

RAF Intelligence claimed that production of diesel engines at the M.A.N. Factory was held up for several weeks but post-war investigation proved otherwise. Not only was the damage slight (five of the bombs had failed to explode), but the casualty rate was unacceptably high. Of the eighty-five men who took off that afternoon, thirty-seven were killed and twelve ended up in prisoner of war camps. Amongst the latter was John Sherwood who survived by nothing short of a miracle when his aircraft hit the ground in a ball of flame. Still strapped in his armoured seat, he was catapulted through the cockpit canopy into trees that cushioned his fall. Amazingly, he was almost uninjured; no more than minor burns, cuts and bruises. Later, he admitted that he couldn't remember anything from the moment the aircraft hit the ground to when he found himself in the trees.

Meanwhile, L7575 had had its moment of glory. In such a damaged state, it was declared a write-off, but then there was a change of heart. A few of the new bombers would be needed for training purposes and if possible to repair, L7575 could still be of use. Such was the damage inflicted on it that it would have been beyond the ground crews to effect the necessary repairs so it had to be put in the hands of the civilian contractors. A team from A.V. Roe arrived on the 24th April and started work. This took over a month but was finally completed on the 28th May. It remained with the squadron for a further two months though was never flown on another operation. It was then decided to send it to a training unit and it arrived at HCU 1654 Wigsley on the 3rd August 1942. In the new unit, the code letters 'OF-Y' on the fuselage were changed to 'UG-Q' (*see David Ansell's illustration*).

Corporal Allan Jones had good reason to remember L7575. It was part of 'A' Flight on the Lincoln side of the airfield, where he worked. On a glider-towing sortie it had developed engine trouble and had to land at Old Sarum, near Salisbury. Allan was sent down to make the necessary repairs and fly back to Wigsley in it. At this stage L7575 must have been part of an experiment in which a few Lancasters had been fitted with struts beneath the tail. The idea was to compare their glider towing characteristics with those of the Halifax. In the event, Halifaxes were preferred

However, there were to be two further occasions when L7575 was in much more serious need of attention. It was grounded from the 10th June till the 3rd July and from the 27th July till the 21st August 1943. On both occasions the actual damage and manner in which it occurred are not on record. It's therefore unlikely that any of the crew involved suffered serious injury. However, judging by the length of time it was out of service and the fact that contractors were called in to carry out the work required, indicate severe problems of some sort. We just don't know how much it was regularly used or on what type of exercises and the question remains as to whether the punishment sustained on the Augsburg Raid had left it with an inherent structural weakness.

Eric Williams, Navigator. [Photo: Christina Williams]

Ewan Taylor, Pilot, when he enlisted in 1940.
[Photo: R.A.A.F.]

Albert Rooks, 1943, Flight Engineer, on his last leave. [Photo: Mabel Cooke]

John Thwaite, Bomb Aimer, 1943. [Photo: Bill Thwaite]

Eddie Stock, 1942. [Photo: Martin Joannides]

Tom Green, Wireless Operator, Blackpool, 1941.
[Photo: Harry Green]

Bruce Davies 1943, Rear Gunner.
[Photo: Rob Cheesman]

Eddie Stock, 1943, Mid-Upper Gunner.
[Photo: Peter Joannides]

Bruce Davies 1943, farewell to girlfriend & family in Australia.
[Photo: Andrew Cheesman]

Bruce Davies, Charterhouse, 1943, last photo, with English cousins.
[Photo: Chris Wilson]

*Douglas Cook, Driver, Fire & Rescue,
Upper Heyford, 1943. [Photo: Alan Cook]*

*Tom Green, Farncombe, 1943, last photo,
with his mother. [Photo: Harry Green]*

Ted Porter, who authorised the final flight of Lancaster L7575. [Photo: Jim Logan]

Allan Jones, Engine Fitter, worked on Lancaster L7575 at Wigsley, 1943. [Photo: Malcolm Jones]

Les Wren, local fireman, 'on the front of the hose'.
[Photo: Lesley Chapman]

Mrs Elizabeth Heffer of Warren Farm who died from
shock soon after the crash. [Photo: Phyllis Gregory]

Colney Heath. Mabel Henton, second from right, and A.T.S. girls from the local searchlight unit who hurried to the scene of the accident. [Photo: Linda Storey]

Clem Palmer, bus driver, off duty, who discovered the dying airman. [Photo: Jean Arnold]

John Thwaite's cigarette case, taken from his tunic pocket after the crash. [Photo: Cedric Greenwood]

Wigsley 2004, a bleak landscape with derelict control tower in the distance. [Photo: Malcolm Jones]

Warren Farm 2000, the Lancaster passed over the oak trees and crashed in the field close to the farmhouse. [Photo: Brian Warren]

Tom Green's chess set, returned to his parents after the crash. [Photo: Cedric Greenwood]

Lancaster L7575 from HCU 1654 Wigsley. [Drawing: David Ansell]

THE LANCASTER'S TAIL
NEAR TO WARREN FARM
COLNEY HEATH

View of Warren Farm the morning after the crash. [Drawing: David Ansell]

Tom Green's Signal Class, Blackpool, 1941. (Nicholas Alkemade seated far right) [Photo: Harry Green]

13. The Last Twenty-Four Hours

On the evening of Thursday 21st October 1943, at Wigsley: 'a WAAF Social was held in the WAAF NAAFI, refreshments were provided and music for dancing by the RAF Regiment Band helped the evening to go with a swing' (*ORB*). Thus began the last twenty-four hours for Ewan Taylor, Eric Williams, John Thwaite, Albert Rooks, Tom Green, Eddie Stock and Bruce Davies. Did they go to the Social? Did they go into town or for a drink at one of the village pubs nearby? We just don't know.

Had they listened to the News they would have learned of the death of Sir Dudley Pound, Admiral of the Fleet, under whose leadership the tide had turned against the U-Boat menace in the Atlantic. The previous night, Bomber Command had launched a heavy attack on Leipzig in 'hail, snow and storm', whilst Mosquitoes raided Berlin and targets in western Germany. The Russians were slowly recovering their territory on the Eastern Front. In the latest bulletins they had advanced in the Gomel and Kiev Sectors. They were gaining ground in Melitopol where, in street to street fighting, they had gained several blocks of houses and were another five miles closer to Krivoy Rog in a bridgehead forty miles deep and twenty miles wide. In Italy the Allies were encountering stubborn resistance. The American 5th Army were consolidating positions, their opponents digging in, whilst the British 8th Army had made small gains. In southern Europe the RAF were bombing marshalling yards in Yugoslavia and raiding Axis bases in the island of Rhodes and the Dodecanese. Meanwhile another large contingent of American troops had arrived in Britain, ready for the invasion of France the following year. We were undoubtedly winning the War but ultimate victory was a long way ahead.

By late 1943 Luftwaffe losses were running at about 15% of their total front line force. Their commitments on the Eastern Front, an unbearable drain on their resources, were leaving

---

them short elsewhere, and they had little to spare for attacks on Britain. By October 1943 they were sending over small numbers in swift night time raids that were of little strategic importance but did cause damage and kill people. My father noted: 'the Germans are imitating our Mosquito tactics – fast planes to avoid our fighters and high flying to avoid our gunfire.' It had been going on every night for nearly a week when twelve of their aircraft crossed Kent and Sussex that evening, some getting through to London, whilst in the North, they sent a few over to Hull. We managed to shoot one down, the third that week, but not before damage had been inflicted and several civilians killed.

In Germany, Lou Watson, Bert Cole and Maurice Scarfe were POWs. On completion of training they had been posted to 49 Squadron that April but were shot up on a raid to Mannheim on the 10th August and baled out over the Black Forest. The whole crew survived unscathed, but were to spend the next twenty-one months in captivity. Back in England, Johnny Kirkup, Jim Logan, Bill Pearson and crew were settling into their new quarters at 207 Squadron Spilsby where they'd reported during the day. Ewan and his crew, on their last night at Wigsley, would almost certainly have known that they were about to be posted to 467 Squadron RAAF at Bottesford. After so long at the Conversion Unit and all the previous training, one can imagine their mixed feelings of anticipation and anxiety, as they were about to go operational.

They woke up on Friday to a fair morning that grew cloudy as it progressed into a thundery afternoon with rain in the evening. Britain, in fact, was situated between two weather fronts: a stationary depression off the Hebrides that was filling up, and another over North East Spain moving quickly north-east and deepening. There were predictions from the Met Office of thundery showers or more persistent rain with localised fog.

After a relatively quiet night on Thursday when eleven Mosquitoes had returned safely from bombing targets at Emden, Dusseldorf and Dortmund, Bomber Command had elaborate plans for their next attack. The principal target was to be the railway system and the three Heinkel factories at Kassel, for which they were to mass 322 Lancasters and 247 Halifaxes. There was to be a diversionary raid on Frankfurt by 28 Lancasters and 8 Mosquitoes. A number of other small raids were planned, and some mine laying off the Dutch coast.

During the day at Wigsley, besides ground training, eleven crews practised circuits and landings, whilst three went for bombing practice on long cross-countries. Ewan and crew would have been told that they were "on" that night. How did they spend their last day? A few possessions returned to their families tell us little enough. Tom Green carried a pocket chess set about with him. On the back is his rank and service number from the time he enlisted as an Aircraftsman 2nd Class until his promotion to Sergeant. A cigarette case was found on John Thwaite's body (*see photograph*). From a photo, we know that Eddie Stock was a pipe smoker and one of his personal effects was a primitive form of petrol lighter. Bruce made things, like the model of a Lancaster, carefully carved out of wood. Not much to go on, but they must have found something to while away the hours.

But, whilst all, so far, was routine at Wigsley, tragedy had struck elsewhere, even before nightfall. Sgt Ian Hayward, son of the local bobby at Hunsdon, Herts, and formerly a carpenter and joiner, was training as a pilot at 14 O.T.U. Market Harborough. On this day the twenty-year-old was flying a Wellington from the satellite airfield at Husbands Bosworth. According to the ORB: 'he had been recalled from the bombing range and when in the neighbourhood of the airfield dived into the ground from a height of 1500 feet. It is assumed that the pilot allowed the aircraft to get out of control and had insufficient height in which to recover. All five of the crew were killed. The aircraft was Cat.E.' (i.e. a total write-off).

Back at Wigsley, flights had been organized for the night. One crew was to practise circuits and landings whilst five others, including Ewan's, were to do their 'Command Bullseye' exercise prior to operational posting. The ORB stated that this was their 'final exercise'. It was to have included Infra Red Bombing, Fighter and Searchlight Cooperation. The flight was authorized by Squadron Leader Edward Leach Porter (*see photograph*). Jim Logan and Bill Pearson, who both flew with him as a Wing Commander the following year, don't remember him at Wigsley and there's no record in the ORB of his posting, in or out, during the months of September and October, but he must have done a short spell there, "resting" from Ops.

By the evening, the weather had seriously deteriorated. My father wrote: 'it is raining fast now and has been for some hours.' That was down in Godalming, Surrey, but it obviously wasn't much better at Wigsley. The crews were briefed on the course to be taken with location of turning points, but such were the weather conditions that the Infra Red Bombing and Fighter Cooperation were cancelled. Only Searchlight Cooperation was possible. Why wasn't the exercise postponed? It seems that the decision must have been influenced by the urgency at this time of month to produce a full quota of operational crews. Moreover, the bombing campaign was costing dear in men and aircraft. Sixteen Lancasters had been lost over Leipzig three nights previously.

Meanwhile, Johnny Kirkup and crew were on their second day at Spilsby. 207 Squadron were to join the planned attack on Kassel. It provided a good opportunity for the new pilot and navigator to each fly "second dickey" as the RAF called it, which was to accompany an experienced crew to observe what was going on. It was common practice at the time and a good method of introducing new crews into an operational squadron. Johnny was to fly with Squadron Leader McDowell, a Canadian who had joined the RAF, and Jim Logan with Pilot Officer Barnett whose crew had already completed about fifteen operations. As the autumn evening closed in, airfields in eastern England resounded to the roar of aircraft engines as hundreds of heavy bombers took to the skies for Germany. As their two Lancasters took off at 1750, Johnny and Jim were about to get their first, and in one case, only, taste of operational flying.

Over in France, the Luftwaffe were about to mount yet another of their small raids. By this stage in the War the RAF had developed a fairly sophisticated system of defence, which was already inflicting regular casualties amongst the German intruders. For this they had two twin-engined night fighters, the Beaufighter and the Mosquito. The Beaufighter was the first of its kind to be equipped with radar. It was eventually superseded for home defence by the faster Mosquito, introduced in mid-1942. In 1943 there were squadrons of both types operating. They had a crew of two, pilot and radar operator. Ground radar stations operated in sectors to detect enemy aircraft. They would vector the fighter in the direction of an aircraft entering their sector. When the fighter had drawn close enough to the intruder it could be picked up on the fighter's radar. The fighter's operator would then guide his pilot towards the intruder until he could establish visual contact and manoeuvre his aircraft into a suitable position to open fire. Four deadly Hispano 20mm cannon would rip into a bomber's fuselage and cause deadly havoc in a matter of seconds.

The historian Sebastian Remus, who has made a study of German documents including the 22nd October, says that 80% of Luftwaffe records were destroyed at the end of the War, so details of their raid this Friday evening are very sketchy. A report from German Naval Command states that their force consisted of seven bombers and eleven night fighters. The bomber unit was from Kampfgeschwader 6, a squadron in Luftflotte 3, because according to another report on aircraft losses, one of this squadron was shot down by a night fighter.

The identity of their night fighter unit is not known and the targets they were detailed to attack are not specified in their records. German Naval Command states that one bomber had to abort and that another was overdue. It says that the low cloud base obscured vision of bombing effects, but a report from the Armed Forces Supreme Command translates: 'fast-moving bombers flew right over London in the night of October 22 and achieved direct bomb hits on the set target areas.' A reason for this apparent contradiction can be seen in 'Incoming Reports from all Armed Forces'. This mentions two Pathfinder Junkers 88 S, adding: 'green and white marking flares were used, similar to those deployed by the enemy Pathfinders.' (*Translator: Angela Ladd*). It isn't really clear whether this related to the Thursday or Friday-night attack, but perhaps the previous report of 'set target areas' applied to the flares that were dropped, the bombers then accurately bombing these markers.

Apart from the two Pathfinders, there's no mention in these reports of the types of aircraft used. The Junkers 88 S was a recent modification involving a more powerful engine, and by removing a turret and reducing the crew from four to three, a sleeker fuselage. This made it faster and more manoeuvrable. According to Sebastian Remus, Kampfgesshwader 6 was probably operating with Junkers 88 Bombers, the standard version having a crew of four; pilot, bomb aimer, rear gunner and wireless operator. The fighters could have been Messerschmitt 110 or 410, Junkers 88 or Focke-Wulf 190. Although, when operating over Germany, they were employed in a defensive role as night fighters, they were also capable of carrying bombs and were used on these intruder raids for ground attack. In other words, they would be classed as fighter-bombers. Number of crew varied from one, in the Focke-Wulf up to three in the Junkers. They were all heavily armed with cannon. Their latest aircraft, the ME 410 had come into service earlier that year. With a crew of two, its cannon could cripple or destroy any allied bomber in seconds.

Reporting this raid the following evening, my father wrote: 'raiders crossed Kent and Sussex Coast and reached Home Counties, East Anglia and London Area. Damage and some fatal casualties.' According to a report from Hertfordshire County Council's Air Raids Precautions Department for the 22nd October: 'a high explosive bomb fell in a field on Netherfield Farm, Colney Street. No damage or casualties'. This indicates that at least one intruder got to the St Albans area, probably targeting the Handley Page, Radlett (Halifaxes) or de Havilland, Hatfield (Mosquitoes).

On the night in question, my father noted: 'we had an alert at 7.20 and the all clear went at 8.30.' These times and German reports of their aircraft numbers are pretty well confirmed by the ORB for 85 Squadron who were flying Mosquitoes out of West Malling: '18.35-20.20 hrs, eighteen enemy aircraft operated from France to the Home Counties and parts of East Anglia. Eight penetrated to the London Area. F/O Thomas gave a dinner party at the Devonshire Club, London, which was attended by F/L Molony, to celebrate his 21st birthday. The dinner took place during an air raid to the accompaniment of A/A guns.'

Earlier, back at West Malling, F/O Shaw and F/O Owen had taken off at 1835 on patrol. They were amongst four Mosquitoes from 'A' Flight who were to encounter 'appalling' weather conditions. Over Kent, there was cloud from 600-1800 ft, with 'icing in cloud and much static'. On the same base, the Canadian 410 Mosquito Squadron also sent out four aircraft on patrol, amongst them F/Lt Jackson and F/O Murray who took off at 1845. Despite the weather, other stations had managed to get their crews airborne, amongst them, Mosquito Squadrons 157 at Hunsdon and 605 at Bradwell Bay. Nine aircraft took off from Bradwell Bay, but it should have been ten. The ORB notes: 'F/O Muir, our Assistant Navigation Officer distinguished himself by falling into a four foot ditch and immersing himself and his maps and charts in 2 ft. of water while going out to fly with S/Ldr Heath. Their sortie was cancelled as their inter-com would not work, this being traced down to wet R/T plugs as a result of his bath.'

Meanwhile, ground control had put F/Lt Jackson and F/O Murray from 410 Squadron RCAF onto a suspected enemy aircraft. They watched on the screen as the Mosquito followed the contact. Then, just after 1957 hrs: ' the plot faded and was completely lost.' Aircraft and crew had disappeared and were subsequently never found. The ORB noted: 'F/Lt Jackson was "B" Flight Deputy Commander and the loss of this crew will be keenly felt by every member of the Squadron.'

At about 19.40 hrs F/O Shaw and F/O Owen of 85 Squadron were: 'vectored towards an outgoing raid at a height of 20,000 ft. Contact was soon obtained and at 19.47 hrs he announced he had a visual on the target. At 19.48 hrs the Controller at Wartling told F/O Shaw that he was only five miles from France. Almost immediately F/O Shaw announced in an excited voice that he had "got it". This was the last transmission received and at 19.51 hrs the blips of the two aircraft faded from the G.C.I. tubes at a point approximately 8-10 miles N.E. of Le Touquet. RDF plots traced an aircraft out to sea near Ostend, which might have been F/O Shaw. It is possible that F/O Shaw shot the E/A' (*enemy aircraft*) 'down and his own aircraft was either hit by bits of the E/A or he may have been hit by the rear gunner, or he may have been hit by flak' (*ORB*). In the event, Shaw survived. He must have either bailed out after crossing the coast or crash-landed his Mosquito a few miles from Le Touquet. News of his capture and internment subsequently came through. Sadly, his radar operator, Owen, was killed, probably by return fire from the rear gunner.

The German bomber involved must be the one listed in the Luftwaffe record of lost aircraft. Though it states 'over England', this must refer to the operation rather than the actual location of the crash. According to this report, the bomb aimer, Unteroffizier (*Sergeant*) Kurt Emmert and wireless operator, Obergefreiter (*Corporal*) Kurt Abramowski, baled out without permission. There are three columns headed, 'Dead', 'Wounded', 'Missing'. Both these men are listed under 'Missing'. No one else in the crew is listed. It would seem that these two had jumped when their aircraft was under attack, still several miles out to sea. The pilot and gunner must have bailed out over land or crash landed their aircraft and survived. As the report is dated the 4th November, and Emmert and Abramowski had yet to be found, it looks as if they suffered the fate, like Jackson and Murray, of so many who just disappeared without trace.

14.   The Final Moments

'Some very bad blackouts in this road. Told one chap about it at 8 o'clock'. Thus wrote my father who was blackout warden for the road where we lived and did his stint of fire watching from the roof of the local school. Back at Wigsley those off duty were filing into the station cinema to watch a Canadian Salvation Army Unit film called "Lucky Jordan".

Meanwhile, Ewan and his crew had been flying for the best part of an hour. After study of the Meteorological Office weather reports, Chris Wilson writes: 'to summarise, L7575 was flying in thick cloud at all heights, maybe with mist or fog below and it was raining nearly everywhere. They would have seen very little.' Well over a hundred of the large force of heavies that had set out for Kassel had been obliged to turn back due to icing. Such were the weather conditions that the following day C-in-C Leigh Mallory sent a signal to his night fighter stations: 'the number of sorties flown against the enemy last night under appalling weather conditions reflects the greatest credit on all concerned. My heartiest congratulations.'

We don't know the scheduled route of Ewan's final flight. The ORB records the crash as being near Watford: 'due to causes unknown'. Ted Porter, under questioning at the inquest, said that: 'it would be in the vicinity of St Albans', as if it was in the right area according to the flight schedule. He stated that L7575's wireless equipment was in order and signed by the tradesman. The plane maintained silence but in any case it wasn't usual for an aircraft to keep in touch with base. However, if there was an alert: 'plane is communicated with by wireless'. As Tom Green, the wireless operator, did not communicate with Wigsley, we can assume that they had no prior warning of any problems, such as mechanical failure etc.

There's some discrepancy in the various records on the actual timing of the crash, but it was probably a little before 8 p.m. when Ted Stebbing, a young medical laboratory scientist, heard the aircraft. At the time he was living in Ormesby Drive, on the western outskirts of Potters Bar (*see Appendix 1 map for location of witnesses*). In his book, 'Diary of a Decade', he wrote: 'the air-raid warning was early tonight. Heavy gunfire close at hand and a plane buzzing around made us a little uneasy. We went and had a look outside but there was nothing to see. There was silence for a while, then some more gunfire farther away followed by a zooming noise and a bump, which put the wind up us. It sounded as though a plane had been brought down. Mrs H. said: "it sounds as though we're in for a night of it". I said: "perhaps that's finished it now". She went outside and spoke to a neighbour. She came back and said everybody was outside talking. Not long afterwards the "All Clear" went.'

One of the first to see the aircraft was Joan Francis. Aged twenty-three, she was with two other Land Army girls, looking out of an upstairs window at Shenley Lodge in the direction of North Mymms. 'We saw this plane on fire. It was crossing from right to left over Redwell Wood. We all cheered because we thought it was a German plane that had been hit.'

John Varty, his brother, Will, and Bill Surridge were looking out from Tyttenhanger Farm. Bill, a twenty-three year old farm worker in the Home Guard recalls how: 'the plane was on fire as it broke through clouds from the direction of Barnet. It didn't seem to be travelling particularly fast.'

David Ansell lived at 32 Peters Avenue, London Colney. He writes: 'on the night in question, my father, a home guard, was on patrol in the area covering the River Colne to the Bell Public House. I was nine years of age at the time and had a huge interest in aircraft, London Colney lying between Radlett (Handley Page) and Hatfield (de Havilland), where my father was employed as an inspector.'

David was up in a front bedroom. 'I had heard what I believed to be a Lancaster flying low, near to our village. On arriving home after duty, I heard my father say to my mother, "I've heard that one of ours has come down at Colney Heath".

Ralph Howell, aged ten, lived at 21 Napsbury Avenue, near David, and was also up in his bedroom. He writes: 'living in a village situated between two airfield factories, it was not surprising that the attentions of the Luftwaffe became a regular feature. Their presence was always obvious by the sound of the irregular throb of their discordant engine noise. We grew adept at aircraft recognition, even as small boys, by sound as much as by sight. During one October night, an overcast sky and some rain falling, I heard an aircraft sound, a heavy multi-engined throb, labouring, but definitely not a "Gerry", and I thought, "that's a Lanc".'

Jim Butters, a young lad approaching the age of fourteen and his elder brother, John, a seventeen-year-old de Havilland apprentice lived at 2 Woodland Drive, on the eastern outskirts of St Albans. They heard the sound of an aircraft approaching and went outside to listen. It was unmistakeably the four Merlin engines of a Lancaster. Though above cloud level as it passed by, their keen ears detected the possibility that all was not well.

Three miles to the northeast of them, in Hatfield, an anonymous correspondent, then sixteen years of age, and styling himself or herself as 'A.N. Other', writes: 'On the night in question, I, with two friends (now deceased) was crossing the Barnet Bypass at the Green Lanes/Lemsford Road Junction on our way to Green Lanes School Youth Club. Suggesting about 1900 – 2000 hours. Not certain if an air raid warning was active. Pitch dark, cloudy night, when a glow dispersed in the clouds and came brighter as the glow left the clouds. A cheer went up from others in the night gloom, thinking a German had been shot down, to subsequently find out with much regret, the object was one of our aircraft, crashing on Colney Heath farmland about three crow miles away.'

The stricken aircraft was even seen from Welwyn Garden City. Ed Kean was cycling down Guessens Road on his way to visit a friend. Aged sixteen and still at the local grammar school, he was very keen on aircraft and in the ATC, which automatically put him in the RAFVR. He was called up into the RAF on his eighteenth birthday just three months after the War.

Suddenly he saw the aircraft burst out of the clouds somewhere to the south: 'it was in a nosedive and on fire. With the dark of night and with no lights around because of the blackout imposed in those days I could very clearly see that it was a four engined bomber as it was illuminated by its own burning flames. A very dramatic picture, which I shall never forget.'

Within about three minutes the Lancaster was back over St Albans. By this time, the Butters boys were out at their front gate and now they saw the burning aircraft as it dived down to a low altitude through the cloud cover, some distance to the south of where they were standing.

Less than half a mile to the east, Derry Pickering, aged nine, lived at 11 Wynchlands Crescent. He writes: 'Mum and Dad worked at de Havillands just down the road from us. Dad was also in the Home Guard and a street firewatcher with my Mum. Our street had a rota and neighbours took it in turns to fire watch under the watchful eye of Mr Ritchie, our local ARP Warden. It was about 8 p.m. and Dad was out in our back garden doing his stint as a firewatcher. I was with my Mum and two sisters in the back room. Suddenly, Dad came rushing in telling us to come into the garden. We were just in time to see a large aeroplane, very low and completely on fire, its engines making a loud coughing, spluttering noise. I would say it was not more than 60 – 75 yards to the south of us and no higher than 300 – 400 feet. Other neighbours had come out in the meantime and we were all cheering, thinking it was a German bomber. Shortly after, there was an explosion and a flash and I remember my Dad saying that it looked as if it had come down over Colney Heath way. A lot of the neighbours met out in the street to chat and laugh about it, still assuming it was a German plane. Only in the morning when my Dad came in, did we learn that it was an English bomber and all on board had perished. I remember my Mum and Sister crying and saying about how we had all cheered when we thought it had been a German plane.'

Back to the night in question and next to see the plane was Jack Last, aged seventeen, who was by the crossroads at the Horse Shoes, Smallford: 'I was walking with a mate towards Smallford Station. We had just entered Station Road when we heard this plane. We couldn't see it because the cloud was too low that night but we could tell from the sound that it was in real trouble. We quickly jumped under the hedge on the side of the road where the allotments were, until it had passed over. As I recall we never heard the crash.'

Peggy Phillips, aged thirteen, lived near Smallford Farm on Colney Heath Lane: 'I was standing at the front door with my mother, aunt and uncle, and saw the plane going over to the left of the house in flames. It was flying level but seemed quite low as it narrowly missed a big oak tree that grew nearby. It was moving very fast in the direction of Colney Heath where it came down.'

Keith Canfield, aged eleven, his older brother Denis, aged fifteen and their parents lived at 30 Sleapshyde Lane and were in the back garden facing south towards Colney Heath. They had heard the sirens going and seen the searchlights. Keith has vivid memories of the low flying aircraft on fire as it came over in a shallow dive just to the west of them. 'On further thought, it seemed that the pilot was doing his best to keep it airborne', he reflects. They could see the fire of the burning plane after it crashed, the exploding ammunition and tracer bullets shooting into the air. At the time they didn't realise it was one of our bombers.

Jim Wild was a schoolboy of eight at the time. 'We lived in the cottage next to Highfield Hall, near Tyttenhanger, which must be a mile or so, as the crow flies, from Colney Heath. My father and I were watching from the front door of the house when the plane came across from the left, very low and in flames, then disappeared behind some trees. I only saw it for about four seconds. It was about half to three quarters of a mile away as I remember it. I can't remember hearing it crash, but it was a very noisy night.'

Harry Harrop aged eight, lived just down the road from Jim Wild. 'It was bedtime. I was indoors with my older brother and sister. Our father, who was outside the front door at the time, called us all out to come and see what had happened. The plane had just crashed and I shall never forget the sight as we went outside. The whole sky was lit up with an orange glow.'

Much closer, in fact, dangerously closer, were Cynthia Bush, aged fourteen, her sister, Celia, and her mother. They lived in the village of Colney Heath. Off the High Street, opposite Wistlea Crescent, a gravel track led down to a tarmac shed where her father worked. Their bungalow faced the track just as it left the High Street. Cynthia said: 'my sister and I had come out of the house. I was sitting in the privy at the bottom of the garden when the plane came over, so didn't actually see it. My sister was in the garden and my mother had come out to call us in. I rushed out into the garden and heard the plane hit and saw a big glow in the sky after it had crashed and there, on the other side of the gravel track, was the wing of a plane, only a few feet away. There was something flashing and exploding on the wing and our father told us not to go near it. Later an air force man came to make it safe and told my father it was for cutting balloon cables.'

Peter Garwood, balloon historian, explains: 'Cable cutters were fairly standard by 1942-3 on both German and British aircraft. At specific points on a wing's leading edge there would be a notch. If an aircraft's wing struck a barrage balloon cable, the cable would slide along into the notch. As it did so it would cause a large cartridge to fire and throw a hardened chisel of steel to sever the cable. Certainly they would be a source of secondary explosion and fire on impact with the ground.' The Bushes were lucky to escape uninjured.

So was Bob Arnold, aged sixteen. On the opposite side of the High Street, in Wistlea Crescent, he had just left his home at No.8. 'I was walking to my Nan's at No.21 when I saw this plane. It was like a ball of fire coming from the direction of Colney Heath Lane, crossing over the bypass and heading for the Church. How it missed the Church I don't know, it was so close. I thought it was going to crash at any moment. I was scared, I can tell you, and ran the last few yards up to my Nan's pressing myself up against the wall of her house. But, the plane passed over heading towards the Warren. After it crashed I walked up Church Lane to Park Gate Corner and saw in the distance the glow of the burning plane. It was pitch black across the Heath, so I went no further.' And a good thing he didn't, as there was live ammunition exploding from the burning wreck.

Also in Wistlea Crescent, Ernie Ralph, was on duty as an air raid warden. He made a statement to the police three days after the crash and later gave evidence at the Inquest. In his statement he said: 'on Friday, 22/10/43, I was outside 34, Wistlea Crescent, Colney Heath, as an Air Raid Warden. An air raid was in progress and gunfire had been heavy. About 8 p.m. I heard the engine of an aeroplane approaching from a north westerly direction. The engines seemed all right, then the engine shut off and then opened out with a terrific roar. There was then a reddish glow above the clouds. I then saw the plane come through the clouds on fire and I could see the full outline of the plane. The plane came down in a spinning dive at a terrific speed, full alight and heard it hit the ground with a thud just south of Colney Heath. It lit the whole place up. After it hit the ground, I could hear what appeared small ammunition exploding. When the plane was coming down, I could see parts of the plane falling apart. It was raining slightly at the time and was cloudy; there was very little wind blowing from the south and there was a slight ground mist. As the plane was coming down, I saw what I thought to be two small lights floating down slowly away from the plane in a westerly direction. Previous to first hearing the plane, there was gunfire in the direction of Harpenden and Luton.'

His evidence at the Inquest was somewhat different. ' I live at 16 Wistlea Crescent, Colney Heath, and am a hairdresser. On Friday 22nd October 1943 about 8 p.m. I was standing at the east end of Wistlea Crescent. I heard a plane hovering round and gunfire in all directions. I heard debris falling and then a terrific roaring of a plane. There was a red glow above the clouds and then the plane dived through the clouds in a spiral spin. The plane was afire and I heard it thud as it struck the ground and the bursting of what appeared to be small ammunition. I was on warden's duty at the time. Plane appeared to come north west and over towards south east.

Gunfire was particularly heavy. Did not see shell bursts. Too much clouds and it was raining. Debris fell within ten yards of me. Boot found in garden next door. Seats found in gravel pits. Oxygen mask was also found.'

The 'terrific roar' described by Ernie Ralph was no exaggeration. The sound to those nearby must have been deafening. Phyllis Wills lived at 1 Waterworks Cottages in Roestock Lane, where her father had been the District Water Inspector until he was called up, subsequently captured and spent the rest of the War in a P.O.W. camp. She remembers: 'as a child of ten, with my brother, seven, and my mother, we all stood petrified in our kitchen as we heard the plane approaching and pass over the house very low, then shortly after we heard the explosion'. Their kitchen faced southwest, towards Warren Farm, but in actual fact, half a mile from the aircraft's true flight path as it crossed over the High Street near the eastern end of Wistlea Crescent and sped on down to the Heath. However, the thunderous sound of that roaring dive could have frightened any of the villagers into thinking that the plane was about to crash into their houses, and the Wills, like most families that evening, thought it was a German aircraft that had been shot down.

Closest to the actual scene of the crash were Phyllis Heffer, aged eighteen, her mother (*see photograph*), and her uncle, 'Gus'. They lived at Warren House Farm (*now known as 'Warren Farm'*) on the outskirts of Colney Heath. Augustus Heffer gave a statement to the Police two days later: 'I am a farm labourer and reside at Warren House Farm, Colney Heath. On Friday 22nd October 1943 at about 7.30 p.m., I was standing outside my house when I heard an aircraft flying. I could not see the plane or any lights on the plane, when suddenly the whole sky lit up and I saw the plane crashing on fire and the plane fell in a field about 100 to 150 yards from where I was standing. There was an air raid warning at the time. There had been gunfire, but when I heard the plane, it was quiet. It was a very dark night and raining. I did not go across to the plane.'

Phyllis had come home for a couple of hours to be with her mother: 'I was on a late night pass from where I worked in St

Albans'. She explained how her father was out fire watching at Salisbury Hall, London Colney, where he worked for de Havilland, her sister had gone to the doctor's and her brothers were away: 'Mum decided it was time to do the blackout curtains upstairs. When she got to the top of the stairs she saw what she described as a "ball of flame" coming straight towards the house. By the time she had got down, the plane had crashed, just in the field, over the tops of the oak trees (*see photograph of oak trees etc. taken in 2000*). My mother and I went outside without coats on. The first person to arrive was Fred Allen, "Pedlar", as we called him. A friend of the family, he came to see if Mum was all right.' Mr Allen's arrival at 9 p.m. enabled Phyllis to return to work where she was due to resume at 9.30: 'I cycled to work, it was not raining then, there was a raid on, but mostly London way. When I went home on Saturday morning, there were guards placed where anyone was likely to try and get to the crashed plane. They tried to stop me from going past them, but as I told the sentry, I would like to get to my bed as I had been at work all night.'

The Police at Barnet were phoned. Inspector Harold Harris made a statement that night: 'on Friday 22nd October 1943 at 8.07 p.m., in response to a telephone message received to the effect that an aircraft had crashed near Colney Heath, I went to Warren House Farm, Colney Heath, and in a field, saw that a four-engine Lancaster Bomber had crashed and was on fire. With other police officers I made an immediate search for the crew and I was present when four of the bodies were found; (1) Sergeant Rooks 1623561, (2) Pilot Taylor 16482, (3) Sergeant Stock 1812793, (4) Sergeant Thwaites 1510800. Parts of the aircraft was found scattered over a wide area. On Saturday 23rd October 1943 at about 12 noon, I was present when two more bodies were found; Pilot Officer (Navigator) Eric Williams 134704 and Sergeant Davies 417460. At the time of the crash it was a very dark night, raining, and visibility was very poor. The air raid alert had been sounded and gun fire had been heavy in the district.'

More details were revealed in his evidence, some days later, at the Inquest: 'I am Sub-divisional Inspector, Barnet

Police Station. At 8.07 p.m. on 22nd Oct 1943 I was informed that plane had crashed in St Albans District. I attended with other officers arriving at 8.25 p.m. An air raid alert was in progress. It was raining heavily. I saw blazing plane. Firemen were in attendance. Ammunition was continually exploding. I was present when four bodies were recovered fifty to a hundred yards from the wreck. Dr Wilson attended. On 23rd October I was present when two further bodies were recovered; one from a farmyard and one in the tail of the plane. I was present on 26th Oct 1943 when the body of the seventh man was recovered from the front of the plane. Bodies removed to the City of St Albans Mortuary. Debris was distributed over a wide area. I communicated with the Air Ministry. Plane was on its back. Bodies recovered were identified by discs and papers found on them.'

One of the local fire brigade mentioned by the police inspector was Les Wren (*see photograph*). His daughter, Marie, a school girl at the time, remembers: 'my Father was a fireman and was on duty that night at Colney Heath Fire Station, which was situated opposite the Cock Public House, so he was one of the first on the scene. I remember him saying there were bodies on the trees in the orchard. He was on the front of the hose and he said bullets kept exploding all round. When he came home his legs were black and blue where he had been taking the pressure of the hose.'

Jack Deuxberry was an engine driver for the St Albans Fire Brigade. When he arrived on the scene there was still a lot of scattered wreckage alight, but the main fire was in the fuselage. They set about putting out the smaller fires and containing the burning fuselage. For such work they were designated as "volunteers", as it was a dangerous situation, but now they were faced with an even more hazardous task. The chief fire officer called them all round and asked for further volunteers. There were a number of small bombs still in the bomb racks of the smouldering aircraft that had to be taken out. As the plane was on its back this would have involved climbing on to the top of the fuselage to get into the bomb bay. Jack stepped forward and was amongst those who carefully got them out and gently placed them in a waiting lorry. The chief officer had hinted that for such a dangerous task there would be medals awarded and the men went home very relieved and optimistic, as they had accomplished the job without mishap (*information on Jack Deuxberry from Derry Pickering, who worked with him after the War*).

Two miles to the northwest, Arthur Allen was at the Head Quarters of 'C' Company Herts Home Guard at Oaklands Institute of Agriculture. 'We were stationed in what at the time was known as the "Dairy", sleeping in the upper section. I, along with two other men, was on guard outside the main door, which faced southeast. It was a dark night. As we were talking we were drawn to a flash to the southeast followed by a sound I can best describe as "wumph", followed by white lights rising to about forty feet. Armed with P17 Rifles, each with five rounds of ammo, we set off across the fields towards the Hatfield road. At first we were going to make our way along the road to a pill box near the Horseshoe crossroads, but when we realised the lights were further south, we took the track through Butterwick Wood (*now built over*) to a level crossing over the railway and then continued southeast. We were drawing close to the North Orbital Road where the lane turns off into Colney Heath Village. All we could see was exploding ammo and as we had now got to the boundary of our operational area and didn't seem to be getting close to the incident, we turned back.'

The 'flash' they saw occurred as the plane finally crashed, and the 'wumph' they heard, was as it set alight the remaining fuel. The 'white lights rising to about forty feet' were the tracer bullets of the aircraft's .303 Browning machine guns, set off by the heat and fire. Some of the exploding ammunition travelled quite a distance. Enid Roberts of Butterwick Farm (*no longer in existence*) was in her garden at the time and rushed indoors to tell her husband, Sidney, what was happening. Their daughter, Nancy, remembers: 'Father, who was in the Home Guard, then got on his bike to go and see where the plane was likely to land. He got as far as the North Orbital, now the A 414, and had to dive in a ditch, as there were bullets flying all around, pinging off the road from the guns in the aircraft as it burnt. He heard the crash and saw the debris flying all around. He continued on after the crash and saw as he was cycling up the village that the plane had come down at the back of the Warren.'

Bill Surridge and the Varty brothers were on the opposite side of the Heath at Tyttenhanger Farm. As the plane struck it had ignited fuel tanks and bullets were flying everywhere. Soon after the crash they tried to approach the aircraft. Crawling up a ditch, they were edging their way towards the burning wreck. 'I reckon we were somewhere between 200 – 250 yards from it before we were driven back by live ammunition exploding in all directions'.

However, there were some who managed to get to the scene of the accident very soon after it happened. Amongst these were A.T.S. (*Auxiliary Territorial Service*) girls from 301 Battery, 93rd Searchlight Regiment, a troop of which was stationed in a field next to the Cock Public House. One of them, Mabel Henton (*see photograph of A.T.S. girls & others*) always remembered the sight of an airman in his leather flying jacket curled up peacefully under a hedge. She later recounted to her daughter, Linda, how he seemed quite unhurt, as if he had fallen to sleep there.

Sadly, the reality was very different, though, despite their multiple injuries, it seems that at least one of them was alive and conscious for a brief while afterwards. Jean Palmer, aged eleven, lived at 63 Tollgate Road, half a mile from Warren Farm. 'That evening I was at my cousin's, Bernice Lewis, two doors down at No.67. There was an air raid on, searchlights shining up into the sky, guns in the distance, a lot of noise. Suddenly Uncle Charlie rushed in. "Quick, get under the table, there's a plane coming down", he shouted, and ducked under the kitchen sink, giving his head an awful bump in the process. I was frightened and told my Aunt I wanted to go home. "Hang on a mo till I turn off the lights", she said, then she let me out the back door.'

'My Dad, Clem Palmer (*see photograph*), was a bus driver. He'd come off the middle shift and was asleep on the sofa when Mum heard the "bang" and woke him up. As I came home he was wheeling out his bike. "I'm going over to Liz (*Mrs Heffer*) to see if she's alright", he said, and off he went.

The Heffers were relations of ours, and Dad spent a lot of time at the farm. Whether he ever saw them that night I don't know. When he got there some people had already arrived. I recall him saying that there was a pond and that there was the body of an airman on the ground. He noticed a movement and as he bent down the young man rolled on to his elbow holding his head in his hand. Dad remembered the shock of dark hair falling over the man's hand. He was trying to say something. It was a woman's name. Though very quiet, Dad heard it twice, quite distinctly: "Eileen, Eileen". Then with a deep sigh the young airman sank back to the ground and lay still. Although I was only eleven at the time I remember when Dad came home how upset he was.'

Arthur Allen remembers Clem Palmer: 'I worked with him at Hatfield London Transport Bus Garage from 1946 until I moved on about 1963, being at the time a LTPB Inspector. Clem was one of the nicest men I had to deal with, but we never talked about the War. Eventually I moved on and lost touch, but he was a great man.'

Bernice Lewis, then aged 12, has a similar account of Clem's experience, except that in her version the airman propped up on his elbow was in Australian uniform lying under a tree. The evidence suggests that this was in the orchard. Clem Palmer knew his way round the farm. The pond was at the top of the orchard. The Australian uniform indicates the pilot, Ewan Taylor. The only other RAAF man, rear gunner, Bruce Davies, never got out of the plane.

Of the four men discovered that night, two fell in the orchard and two in the farmyard. Albert Rooks definitely fell in the orchard. It was through a fruit tree, which had to some small degree cushioned his fall. Apart from a broken nose, he hadn't suffered extensive head injuries like the other three. It's therefore more likely that he might have regained consciousness, if only briefly, after the crash. He was seriously involved with a girl on his last spell of leave only a few days earlier. However, his sole surviving sister is positive that her name wasn't Eileen.

The same also applies to John Thwaite. His brother was quite certain that John's girlfriend had a different name. This leaves Eddie Stock and Ewan Taylor. Unfortunately, despite extensive research, it has not been possible to find any contemporaries with the necessary information.

In his statement to the Police made on the 24th October (*see full post mortem report in Appendices*), Doctor Ronald Edmund Wilson of 54, Holywell Hill, St Albans, said he arrived at the scene at 8.50 p.m. He saw the bodies of the four whom the Police had discovered so far. He subsequently examined them, and the two that were found the following day, in the St Albans City Mortuary. He said: 'all six men had sustained extensive injuries of great severity such as would be caused by an air crash. The injuries in each case would have caused instant death. There was a noticeable similarity in the injuries of Thwaites, Taylor, Stock and Rooks'. However, he noted that Rooks had been less severely injured because: 'his body lay beside a thick branch of a tree, which appeared to have been torn off by his fall'.

By the time of the Inquest all seven men had been accounted for. His evidence reads: 'I saw bodies of seven airmen and examined them all at the City Mortuary and found as stated in my report. Cause of death in each case; severe injuries received in air crash. No other injuries on bodies to suggest they had been received before the crash. Injuries caused by impact of machine with ground.'

So it seems that not one of the crew suffered any injury till the last few seconds of his life. We can only try to imagine the frightening scene within the aircraft. Was it flying high enough for them to bale out? Did they hesitate? Whatever the problem, did it happen too quickly for them to do anything about it? Once the aircraft began to spin out of control there was little hope. Max Hastings ('*Bomber Command*') sums up the statistics: 'the occupants of a stricken aircraft had a one-in-five chance of escaping alive. Fighting the G-forces of a diving or spiralling, uncontrollable descent, they had to ditch the hatches, reach their parachutes and somehow struggle clear before the bomber struck the ground.'

Personal accounts of such an experience are hard to find, simply because few survived to tell the tale, but there is an example in Kevin Wilson's book, 'Bomber Boys', of Pilot Officer Alan Bryett, bomb aimer in a Halifax piloted by Flight Lieutenant Kevin Hornibrook RAAF, shot down over Germany on the 24th August that year. He recalled that the two gunners had already been killed by the night fighter and the pilot had ordered: "Don't bale out" as he was corkscrewing. However, the engineer, navigator and wireless operator only heard the "bale out", as there was obviously no hope, and had jumped. He continued: 'I went up and sat with the pilot. It was quite obvious we weren't going to make it, but then the terrifying thing was that as the plane twisted and turned we couldn't get to the escape hatch. We were being tossed around in the nose of the plane. Eventually Kevin did manage to get to the escape hatch, pulled it open, got hold of me and pushed me out with his feet, shouting: "I'm coming". We knew we were very low. I pulled my ripcord and was only coming down for seconds before I felt what I thought were bushes. In fact I was in a forest of fir trees about 80 feet up. The pilot was all ready to follow me, but as I was up in the trees I saw the aircraft crash in a bit of open ground. It was burning furiously. He didn't get out.'

If they had been shot down in a Lancaster their chances of survival would have been even worse. Peter Jacobs ('*The Lancaster Story*') points out that the survival rate in Halifaxes that were brought down was nearly twice that of a Lancaster. He adds: 'When looking at the individual crew positions, it is possible to assess the chances of each individual crew member. Those at the front of the Lancaster, particularly the bomb aimer, appear to have had a greater chance of escape owing to their being close to the forward escape hatch, whilst those towards the rear of the aircraft had less chance. Statistically, just over 10% of rear gunners in the Lancaster escaped compared to 30% of Halifax rear gunners, and nearly 20% of wireless operators compared to 40% in the Halifax. It is also interesting to note that the statistics of survival rates amongst US B-17 Flying Fortresses and B-24 Liberators operating over Europe by day were more favourable; approximately 50% overall.' When comparing the Lancaster and Halifax, he points out that the rear door in the former was very close to the tail section, which could be hazardous for anyone trying to bale out. The door in the Halifax was further forward and therefore more practicable.

In the case of Ewan and crew, there just isn't enough evidence to form a judgement on whether at least some of the crew could have saved themselves if they had acted immediately. It was up to the pilot to try and hold the aircraft steady for as long as possible to enable his crew to escape, but altitude was also a vital factor. When Peggy Phillips and Jim Wild caught sight of the plane in its last few seconds it was already flying far too low. In those last few terrifying moments they must have realised the inevitable. There wouldn't even have been time to ponder the fact that all those months of intensive training punctuated with periods of waiting, building up the skills and endurance necessary for what they had volunteered to do, had, in a minute or two of misfortune, all come to nothing.

Just over half an hour after Ewan and his crew had plunged to oblivion, a similarly tragic scene was unfolding in Germany. Pilot Johnny Kirkup and navigator Jim Logan, who had just finished their training at Wigsley and been posted to 207 Squadron the previous day, were both flying "second dickey" with their respective Lancaster crews in the main bomber force on the raid to Kassel. At 8.30 Squadron Leader McDowell was over Nettersheim, about twenty miles South-West of Bonn, when he was spotted by Lieutenant Otto Fries of Nacht Jager 1, a squadron from Luftflotte 2. The night fighter shot him down and all were killed, including McDowell's young eighteen-year-old Flight Engineer, Sgt MacNish Porter, and Johnny Kirkup. Johnny had just received his commission as a Pilot Officer. He was only twenty-one and already married. Jim remembers meeting his young wife, Laura. It was a cruel blow for her. It also left his crew without a skipper before they'd even flown one operation.

McDowell's was one of 43 aircraft that night, mostly lost to night fighters: three hundred men, few of whom survived. 7.6% of the force was a high price to pay and yet the raid was considered a resounding success by Bomber Command in terms of the damage it inflicted: 150 industrial buildings, including a factory making V1 bombs and the local Gestapo

Headquarters as a bonus. But, the human price was terrible. The bombing created a firestorm similar to that in Hamburg earlier that year. Services were overwhelmed. More than five and a half thousand died, many trapped in their shelters. More than 60% of the town's living accommodation was lost. A week later, fires were still burning.

'There is a fire to the N.W. not far away that keeps on coming up': wrote my father that Friday night after his stint of fire watching from the school roof in Godalming.

Back at Wigsley it was now 11 p.m. Despite the bad weather the other four aircraft had completed their final exercise and each of their crews were due to be posted to an operational squadron. The warm fug of human occupation and stale cigarette smoke lingered in the empty station cinema. The Canadian Salvation Army film, "Lucky Jordan", had been shown to a packed house and: 'apart from a few technical hitches the show was an entertaining one'.

Lancaster L7575 was overdue. A message was sent. It was not acknowledged.

15.   The Route…

Brian Hayward, aged seven, lived at 1 Sleapcross Gardens, alongside the North Orbital Road, very close to its junction with Smallford Lane. He remembers how quickly the fire engines and ambulances raced to the scene. He was outside his house with a friend Alex Whiffen when the stricken plane screeched overhead. From where they stood it was too misty to see anything of the aircraft, but as soon as it crashed they raced off on their bikes up Park Lane to the Waterworks where Alex's father was the manager. Police Constable Day, the village bobby, and another constable were already there before them. 'You clear off boys', PC Day told them, and so they did, but managed to catch a distant glimpse of the aircraft from the Heath, the following day. It was lying flat on the field. Len Bean, aged seventeen, and a fitter in a factory at that time, went to see what had happened. He remembers the flames. He returned next day and also saw the aircraft lying flat. He wasn't allowed near. Bill Surridge tried to approach the site from Tyttenhangar Farm. 'We only got a little way up the field before we were stopped. It was all cordoned off.' Jimmy Whiting, the present landlord of the Cock Inn, was only a child at the time but remembers seeing the charred remains of the aircraft: 'they put a barbed wire barrier all round the area where the plane crashed.' I asked him if it had nose-dived into the ground: 'no', he said, 'it looked as if it had crash landed'.

No one was allowed near. First, there was the gruesome task of recovering the bodies. According to the official re-ports, four men, Taylor, Thwaite, Rooks and Stock were found at 8.10 p.m. 'in a field at Warren House Farm'. The timing implies that they must have been discovered very soon after the crash by the rescue services, before the Police arrived and forty minutes before Dr Wilson got to the scene. The general-ised location is inaccurate. Phyllis Heffer remembered: 'there were two bodies found in the farmyard, right opposite the back door. There was a high black fence dividing the farmyard from the house. Also, two were found in the orchard by the hen house and where the ground was so soft the imprints of their bodies were there for a long time after the crash.' She said that one of the airmen had fallen through a Codling apple tree near the hen house, at a part of the orchard nearest the house. This must have been Albert Rooks, the flight engineer.

It was not till 12 Noon the following day that Bruce Davies was found in the tail of the plane. It would obviously have been too dangerous to approach the wreckage closely the previous evening and of no help to any still left inside as there was no chance of them surviving. It's this evidence that confirms Bruce as the rear gunner on that flight, whatever his normal position in the aircraft. He must have somehow been trapped in the rear turret, unable to get out. From the medical evidence, he might have been knocked unconscious in the final spinning dive before the aircraft hit the ground.

A quarter of an hour after they found Bruce Davies, the body of Eric Williams was discovered. As with the others, the official report simply states: 'in a field at Warren House Farm'. The Police Inspector, Harold Harris, at the Inquest said: 'in a farmyard', but this vague description is likely to be as inaccurate as in the other official reports. The Doctor had stated that the multiple injuries of the four discovered the previous night were of a similar nature, though those of Albert Rooks were not quite as severe because his fall had been broken by the apple tree. This implies that the manner in which they were thrown from the aircraft was similar. Eric's injuries were different. He had hit the ground from a vertical fall and it would seem that he left the aircraft slightly before the others and therefore, his body was found further away. Though Bill Surridge didn't see the body, he worked on Tyttenhanger Farm, and is therefore more likely to know than anyone else. There's a public footpath crossing the agricultural land in a south-westerly direction from just north of Warren Farm to Tyttenhanger Farm. It is now a featureless part of one large field, but at the time was lined with a shallow ditch and bank beside which were some oak and ash trees and lower growing shrubs. Eric was discovered close to this public right of way.

By the middle of Saturday six out of the seven in the crew had been found. On Sunday my father received a phone call at 1 p.m.: 'Tom missing, believed killed. I went over to see Chas. He and May were very brave. He has taken it very calmly. He is badly hit, poor chap. I have been expecting this news somehow and so has he. I saw Tom last on Sunday Sept 26th.' His diary continues, on Monday: 'went to see Chas. No further news yet.' Tuesday: 'still no news of poor Tom.' Wednesday: 'phone call from May. Tom's body has been found. Poor little chap. 21! Went to Feltham (*the undertaker*) with May and made all arrangements.'

In fact, Sgt Thomas Green, wireless operator, was discovered at 4 p.m. the previous day, Tuesday, in the front of the plane, which, according to the Police Inspector, was on its back. It had taken from the previous Friday evening to find him. Unlike the others, there are no written details of his post mortem examination. It's quite possible that they only discovered his remains when they started to remove the charred wreckage of the plane.

They had a real job collecting up all the debris. Brian Hayward remembers seeing one of the low-loaders getting bogged down in the field. John Carpenter, aged six, of Sleapshyde Lane recalled watching the wreckage being towed away on the 60 ft 'Queen Mary' trailers the RAF used for transporting aircraft fuselage. When he walked to Colney Heath School he remembered seeing a lot of debris, especially round the Wistlea Crescent area and in particular a large piece of fuselage and a black rubber dinghy. On the Saturday morning Bob Arnold's mother discovered the inner lining of an Elsan toilet in the garden of their house at 8 Wistlea Crescent. 'Such a useful find was used for years afterwards as a bucket for chicken corn and later still for nuts and bolts. People didn't chuck things out in those days.'

It's possible to trace the direction the Lancaster took from the location of debris, especially in the later stages (*see Appendix 2: Map for location of debris*). However, there's proof that it was initially heading northwest. Ralph Howell of London Colney writes: 'next morning, a Saturday I think, no school and no holiday, and football in the afternoon. The lads in the road met and we heard that a bomber had crashed nearby during the night. Just how the news arrived, I don't know, but village telegraph was efficient and quick, usually passed on by those men who were in the ARP or Rescue Squad after night duty, or perhaps, the milkman on his very early round. Someone knew the way and we followed on, told that it was in a field at the village of Tyttenhanger, near Small-ford. The lane that led to the crash site was a turning off the North Orbital Road, a road that passed both the edge of Handley Page's and near to de Havillands, between London Colney and Hatfield. We arrived at the junction of Highfield Lane and Tyttenhanger Lane (known as 'Tyttenhanger Green') at about 10.30 a.m. to find a small knot of people aligning a hedge and looking across the field to a small copse of trees where some wreckage was visible. "It's one of ours", someone said. "A Lanc", said another, and as we edged forward, a police sergeant came towards us and told us to stay behind the hedge at the roadside. The grass near the hedge and ditch was long, and the field beyond was ploughed and harrowed. The wreckage was two or three feet high, but not in a solid piece: it was several collective pieces varying in height and perhaps twenty-five to thirty feet long, projecting from the line of trees, so there may have been more. I don't recall smoke, and there was a small group of servicemen or a work party in and around the site, and they appeared to be busy. There was nothing to suggest it was a Lancaster, that is what we were told, and a small object near to the debris and closer to us was identified as a flying boot. We stayed about an hour, unrealistically hoping to get closer, and finally gave up and returned to the village. During the next day or so, a rumour circulated that the aircraft had been shot down by our own side. The origins of that belief was never established, how-ever, I have always believed it to be credible, and always believed that the aircraft was a Lancaster bomber. After a week of school, a few of us returned to the field the following Saturday, to find the wreckage gone.' As it turned out, this location was not where the Lancaster finally came to rest, as these onlookers thought, though this debris undoubtedly came from Lancaster L7575.

Arthur Allen, of the Home Guard at Oaklands on the night of the crash, remembers: 'at about 11 a.m. on a Sunday morning in 1943 on a date unknown, we had been sent out on a test of communications carrying semaphore flags. My platoon went alongside a hedgerow and into a field recently ploughed with stubble still to be seen, i.e. obviously a shallow ploughing. As we crossed the field we came upon a piece of metal about three feet square, with clean-cut edges but buckled through contact with something. The metal was clean, no sign of mud, as if it had recently fallen since the field had been ploughed. Among my squad of eight men were a number who worked at de Havillands and said it was definitely aircraft material. It was painted in a colour that I would describe as between olive green and ochre. A brief search of the area revealed nothing further.' On a roughly drawn map Arthur indicated a position in a field on the northern side of Coopers Green Lane and judging by the distance indicated, a little to the north of Beech Farm. Although this small piece of wreckage can't definitely be proven as part of L7575, it could undoubtedly have been close to its flight path.

Eventually, when the Lancaster turned onto its final course its passage was strewn with wreckage. The morning after the crash, Jack Last, father of the seventeen-year-old of the same name (*see Chapter 14*), was out poaching for rabbits on the most northerly section of Sear and Carter's Nursery, which is just north of the crossroads at the Horseshoes. Here he came across a flying boot. From this point the main parts that the aircraft shed follow more or less in a straight line to the place where it crashed in the field some fifty to a hundred yards west of the farmhouse.

John Butters, the de Havilland apprentice, and his younger brother, Jim, were cycling to see the crash site the following day. They saw a wing tip by the road about 150 yards North of the railway station at Smallford. This had, in fact, come from the port wing. Jim Bacon, who lived nearby in Springfield Road, remembers it well: 'I was fifteen years old at the time and a telegram boy for the Post Office at St Albans. A fragment from the aircraft had floated down onto the roof of Smallford Post Office dislodging a few tiles then clattered down to the ground in front of the building.

It was still there a week later when David Willson, aged 12, of Endymion Road, Hatfield, went to see his grandfather who lived at Colney Heath. David remembers: 'After school the following Friday (29th October) I and one of my classmates took the bus from Hatfield to Smallford Crossroads. We walked down Station Road and saw the wing tip outside the Post Office. It was about six to eight feet in length. We crossed the hump back bridge over the railway and in a field just to the right we saw what looked like either the underside of the aircraft's nose or perhaps the underside of the rear gun turret. We could see further pieces of the aircraft as we walked down Smallford Lane.'

Keith Canfield, of Sleapshyde Lane, like a lot of youngsters, had tried to get on to the Heath to see the plane, but been turned away. However, he did manage to get hold of a little debris. There were gravel pits just to the south of Smallford Station on the west side of Smallford Lane, part of the workings being filled with water. About a hundred yards in off the road, there was debris from the aircraft strewn over the ground, some of it partially submerged in the water. He and his friends managed to get hold of a few smaller bits, but he remembers some were really large: 'as big as an armchair'. It wasn't long, though, before they had to part with their new-found treasures. The Police turned up at Colney Heath School the following Monday and told the children to hand in any debris off the plane to the school.

George Archer, a man in his thirties, was standing outside the factory where he worked, in Camp Road on the eastern edge of St Albans. Earlier, he had seen the aircraft in flames but had a further surprise when he returned home after his shift to find two small pieces of wreckage in his garden at 12 Smallford Lane, just north of the Orbital Road (*information from David Willson*).

A de Havilland apprentice, Bob Robinson, later a Petty Officer in the Fleet Air Arm, was cycling to work the following day for an 0800-1230 shift: 'when I got down to Sleapshyde just past the junction of the Orbital Road and Smallford Lane, on the grass verge was a large piece of aircraft wing, which appeared to me to be the outer wing of a bomber with the aileron missing.' It was lying upside down and on reflection he thought it was the starboard wing tip.

Jim Wild was another youngster who went that Saturday to see what had happened and remembers an engine in the middle of the main road near the Crooked Billet Pub, which is in the High Street beyond the eastern end of Wistlea Crescent. By the time Marie Wren was going to school the following Monday it had been shifted to the grass verge by the roadside. This engine was obviously associated with the wing section that fell near the Bush's house close by. Cynthia remembers the boot mentioned by Ernie Ralph at the Inquest: 'it had the name, "Taylor", in it.' Unfortunately the owner of the boot that fell out at Tyttenhanger and the one at the nursery go unrecorded.

So, by the time L7575 had crossed over the village of Colney Heath it had lost most of one wing, plus a wing tip from the other wing, the rubber dinghy, seen by John Carpenter, which was stowed in the root of the starboard wing and the toilet situated in the rear of the aircraft. At this stage, just seconds before it crashed, the plane was falling apart. When I visited Warren Farm in 2003 the farmer showed me where the next engine came off. This was at the northern end of the orchard, furthest from the farmhouse.

It must have been very close to this point that L7575 crossed the tree-lined boundary. Brian Hayward and his young friends knew the farmland well. They used to go potato picking for the local farmers: 'we would hide one or two in our shirts or even bury one a bit deeper and creep back when it was dark to retrieve it. You had to get what food you could in those days.' He remembers a limb torn from one of the oak trees: 'the plane must have clipped the top of the trees as it came over.'

David Ansell remembers: 'the following morning, after running some errands for Mum and hearing the breaking story of the crash, I borrowed a bike from Jimmy Kaye's sister and cycled over to Colney Heath with the other lads from the village via Bell Lane (*Coursers Road*), late morning. We arrived at a bend in the lane where the field boundary runs along towards Warren Farm. We laid our cycles on the verge and managed to crawl through small gaps in the hedge. The grass was very high and we had difficulty in seeing anything, but in the distance we could see what looked like the tail fins of the Lancaster tilted upwards (*see David Ansell's illustration*). That's as far as we got. There were some military personnel and I believe, policemen, preventing any souvenir hunters or photographers getting too close.' The exact location of the tailplane is difficult to determine. Witness reports are confused. On the official accident card it states, 'tail had failed', listed after 'wingtips' and 'wings near outer engines'. This clearly indicates that the tailplane had come off before the aircraft crashed. If so, it could have only been just before, but it's possible that this took place prior to crossing the oak trees near the top of the orchard.

Like David Ansell, Bob Robinson cycled from London Colney to see the wrecked plane. He remembers: 'On Sunday I rode with my chums Albert Light and Jimmy Kaye over to Colney Heath. We went down Coursers Road turning left by the Bell Public House. We reached Coursers Farm and on the left side of the road the gate into the field was open. Just inside and to the right, rammed into the ground alongside the hedge, was a Merlin engine. Diagonally across the field, maybe fifty yards away along the hedge that bounded Warren House Farm was a second Merlin, covered in earth and oil. We wanted to go over the field towards the crash site but were stopped by a fireman who told us they hadn't been able to get near the remains due to the heat, so we left the scene and never saw the crash site.'

Bill Surridge, who worked on Tyttenhanger Farm, also knew of the engine by the roadside. Up against the hedge at the far end of the field, it was over a quarter of a mile from where the plane crashed, which testifies to the speed that the aircraft was travelling as it dived towards the ground. The two engines that were projected by the plane as it hit would have gone even further had they not been stopped by the field boundaries. The fact that they travelled so far proves that the aircraft's final dive was shallow. If it had been a steep nose-dive they would have been embedded in the ground where the plane struck.

The field in which L7575 crashed is very large. On the south-western side is Tyttenhanger Farm, to which the field belongs. On the opposite side, over a third of a mile away, is 'Warren Farm', as it is now called. The field boundary beside what was the orchard and farmyard of Warren Farm is lined with oaks. The exact location of the crash is difficult to determine but was fairly close to this boundary, as the bodies in the farmyard and orchard were, according to Inspector Harris: 'fifty to a hundred yards from the wreck.'

Peggy Phillips and Jim Wild, as they watched the plane, both noticed how low it was flying. It was a shallow dive in a south-easterly direction. It was just high enough in altitude to cross the tree-lined boundary on the edge of the field, clipping one of the trees as it did so, but in a shallow enough trajectory to 'crash land' as Jimmy Whiting put it, rather than to nose dive into the ground. A straight line between Bob Robinson's two pinpoints, i.e. the wing tip at Sleapshyde just north-east of the main road junction with Smallford Lane and the Merlin engine by the gateway opposite Coursers Farm on Coursers Road shows what I believe to be the direction the aircraft took in its final few seconds. This line crosses Colney Heath High Street near the eastern end of Wistlea Crescent where the first engine was found and crosses over the tree-lined field boundary at the very north-westerly tip of the orchard at Warren House Farm, where the second engine fell off the plane. Crossing the field boundary at this point it continued into the field in a south-easterly direction until it finally 'crash landed' about fifty yards from the farmhouse. If the aircraft had passed directly over the orchard and farmhouse then still have been high enough to fly over the oak trees, its shallow dive would have taken it much further from the farmhouse.

To Mrs Heffer, peering into the darkness out of the window at the top of her stairs she was struck with terror by the sight of that 'ball of flame' as it seemed to be heading straight for the house. In fact, the aircraft was going to miss the house by some margin, but when you look at an approaching light surrounded by darkness it always seems to be heading straight for you. I've been to the top of that staircase and there's no doubt that Mrs Heffer would have clearly seen the aircraft coming from the direction of the village.

The other question, one that we can only guess at, is how the four airmen found on the night of the crash came to be in the orchard and farmyard, to one side of the aircraft's direction and on the other side of the tree-lined boundary from where the aircraft came down. According to Dr Wilson: 'injuries (*were*) caused by impact of machine with ground'. It must be remembered that Ernie Ralph had described the 'spinning dive' and 'spiral spin' of the aircraft in his evidence. As the plane came over the end of the orchard and into the field, it was spinning. It's therefore possible that the men could have been flung sideways rather than forwards in the direction the aircraft was heading, or maybe, forwards but at an angle. Considering the plane landed on its back, is it possible that they could have been thrown out after it struck the ground? And, if that were the case how could they have negotiated the tree lined field boundary in order to end up in the orchard and farmyard?

Isn't it more likely that they were flung out of the aircraft before it struck the ground? From Phyllis Heffer we know that two fell in the farmyard and two in the orchard. Albert Rooks definitely fell in the orchard; his fall broken by one of the trees. We know from his mention of the pond that Clem Palmer was in the orchard when he discovered the airman still conscious. If this was an RAAF man in the distinctive dark blue uniform the Australians wore, it would have been Ewan Taylor, the pilot. That leaves Edward Stock and John Thwaite as the two men in the farmyard. Brian Warren, Honorary Archivist of the Potters Bar and District Local History Society, who did much of the initial research on the crash, went to Warren Farm in 1999 and was shown where one of the airman was found at the foot of a hedge in the farmyard area, in 'full flying kit'. This was undoubtedly the one seen by Mabel Hinton of the ATS searchlight unit, 'in his leather jacket, curled up peacefully under a hedge, as if he was sleeping'. If

Taylor was with Rooks in the orchard, this would have been either Stock or Thwaite.

Taylor, Rooks and Thwaite (pilot, engineer and bomb aimer) were all in crew positions at the front of the aircraft. Stock, the mid-upper gunner, was thrown out with them and had sustained similar injuries. Would he have attempted to reach the rear door, near the aircraft's tail? This exit would have been the closest but might have been impossible due to damage sustained or fire spreading backwards through the aircraft. Perhaps he had managed to struggle forwards to the cockpit area before the aircraft started to spin. It's also possible that for some reason he was in the front turret, rather than the normal mid-upper position. Fighter affiliation had been cancelled that night. Theoretically the gunners, apart from keeping a look out, were only there for the ride. The front turret was just above Thwaite, the bomb aimer, in the nose of the aircraft, close to the main escape hatch. Maybe this was the case, with Rooks, the engineer, and Taylor, the pilot, thrown out from their positions in the cockpit into the orchard and the other two out of the nose into the farmyard. It would explain why each pair landed in a different area. It is also perhaps significant that Harris the Police Inspector listed the casualties they discovered that night in the order, Rooks, Taylor, Stock and Thwaite: the first, we know, in the orchard and therefore probably the second as well, the other two, then, in the yard.

It is, of course, all supposition, but if these men were flung from the aircraft an instant before it crashed, it's even more likely to be so in the case of Williams, the navigator. Unlike the others who were flung to port, he was flung to starboard close to the junction of the footpath with the oak lined boundary that ran down to Warren Farm. Because at this stage the aircraft was slightly higher in altitude and his vertical fall, head first, unimpeded, he had sustained the most horrific injuries of all those flung from the aircraft. As can be imagined, they would have been instantly fatal.

Very positive evidence of the ferocity with which the crew were hurled from an aircraft that could project a Merlin engine for a quarter of a mile, lies in a cigarette case that was recovered from the tunic pocket of John Thwaite (*see photographs*). A strong metal case has been twisted and flattened by its impact with the ground.

Like Davies, who had been trapped in the rear turret, Green never got out of the plane. His position as a wireless operator was towards the back of the cockpit area against the main spar. If he tried to send a message back to base in the last few minutes, it didn't get through. As the plane was coming down, Ernie Ralph, the witness at the Inquest, saw what looked like: 'two small lights floating down slowly away from the plane in a westerly direction'. Could they have been identification flares set off by the wireless operator? Improbable, thinks Geoff Paine, a wartime Wellington pilot. They were more likely to have been set off accidentally by the heat from the burning aircraft.

As for the route of the plane, before the final dive, a clue to this lies in the evidence of Ernie Ralph, the air raid warden at Wistlea Crescent. In his statement to police he says: 'I heard the engine of an aeroplane approaching from a north-westerly direction'. At the inquest he was more specific: 'plane appeared to come north west and then to north and over towards south east.'

'From a north-westerly direction' and 'towards south east' are the same. What he added at the inquest was that before heading south-east the aircraft had altered course. It had, in fact, turned round and was heading back in a similar direction from which it had come. Ted Stebbing was on the western outskirts of Potters Bar. In his book 'Diary of a Decade' he describes how the plane was close at hand and then further away. Joan Francis at Shenley Lodge and Bill Surridge at Tyttenhanger Farm both saw it coming from the direction of Potters Bar. That it was flying northwest is confirmed by the debris discovered near Tyttenhanger Green.

The next part of the aircraft's route is the hardest to reconcile with Ernie Ralph's description, though the basic outline is correct, i.e. that it was heading northwest, then turned round onto a south-easterly course. The problem lies with its exact line of flight from when it passed over Tyttenhanger Green to when it got to Smallford and started on its final dive.

When the Butters brothers eventually saw it break through cloud cover from the front gate of 2, Woodland Drive, on the eastern outskirts of St Albans, Jim writes: 'we were looking approximately due South and the Lancaster travelling more or less East – the latter being very difficult to recall, particularly as it was also diving'. Regarding distance, he adds: 'difficult to judge after all this time, but I would think a bit further away than Hatfield Road.' He later recalled that it had: 'emerged at low altitude, with low throttle'. It had more or less crossed this main road half a mile further on when Derry Pickering and family of 11 Wynchlands Crescent saw it 'going from right to left as we were standing.' He guessed its altitude would have been 300-400 ft at the time and remembered that it was making a 'coughing, spluttering' noise. At this stage it was heading in the direction of Smallford.

So, in order to follow the route outlined by Ernie Ralph, it would have had to turn on to a north-westerly course that took it somewhere near Beech Farm, where Arthur Allen's Home Guard platoon found the piece of wreckage. Also, George Archer, looking north towards Sandridge from his factory on the eastern outskirts of St Albans claimed to have heard it in that area. David Willson, aged twelve, of Endymion Road in Hatfield, remembers the aircraft flying around: 'on the far side (*the west side*) of de Havillands'. Then it altered course again, and it had done so when Ed Kean saw it from Guessens Road, Welwyn, to the south of him, in a 'nosedive' on what he thought was a south-westerly course.

This is the exact direction described by the anonymous 'A.N. Other' who was in Hatfield at the Lemsford Road/Greenlanes junction on the Barnet Bypass: 'the flaming object came from a northerly direction travelling southerly, more or less on the overall line of the Barnet Bypass.' In fact, the main road at this point is heading southwest. Following this course, more or less, would have taken the aircraft to Smallford, where we know from the debris the plane changed direction again, heading southwest to Colney Heath.

However, there's a problem with this simple route outlined by Ernie Ralph. Jim Butters comments: 'what I cannot really believe is that, from the position in which we saw it, with low throttle (spluttering?) engines, the Lancaster would be able to regain height, re-enter cloud and circle round to the north as seen by other witnesses'.

The only conclusion to be drawn is that, in fact, the witnesses in Hatfield and Welwyn did see the aircraft before Jim Butters and Derry Pickering. In order to do this and maintain the general direction that they saw it flying, the aircraft must have crossed back over to St Albans, circled round and turned east towards Smallford crossing its original northerly course in a figure of eight (*see map in Appendix 1*).

The flying boot found in Sear and Carter's Nursery to the north of the Horseshoes crossroads marks the final change of direction from where the aircraft was shedding debris on a more or less south-easterly course to the crash site and beyond.

To sum up the aircraft's route, it would seem that L7575 was heading in a north-westerly direction from somewhere in the region of Potters Bar towards St Albans, which might have been a turning point on the exercise plan. In fact, Ted Porter, their commanding officer at Wigsley, said: 'Plane would be in vicinity of St Albans'. By this time it was already on fire. When the Butters brothers first heard the Lancaster above cloud level it was flying north. It turned round somewhere in the open countryside between St Albans and Welwyn, touching the eastern edge of Hatfield. From there it flew back to St Albans and turned east to Smallford, then abruptly changed on to its final south-easterly course towards Colney Heath. The reason for so many changes in direction is tied up with the cause of the accident and a matter for discussion in the following chapter.

The day after the accident, Ted Stebbing wrote: 'it seems fairly certain that the plane which came down last night was one of our Lancasters, as it crashed not far away and several people said it was. Some people saw it come down in flames and two parachutes bale out. Somebody else said eight men were killed, which would tally up, as there were ten in a crew.'

Ted's knowledge of aircraft matters was obviously not extensive. Or, perhaps, he was confusing the crew of the Lancaster with that of the American B17 Flying Fortress. The 'two parachutes' were almost certainly the 'two small lights' in Ernie Ralph's account, but then he concludes: 'The burning question is: was our plane shot down by our guns?' It was a question many were to ask over the following weeks.

16. …and Cause

On Saturday morning, the 23rd October, Jack Deuxberry[2] of the St Albans Fire Brigade and fellow firemen reported for duty and were ordered out on parade. As they lined up there was anticipation in the air. Out came the fire chief. He had nothing but praise for the way they had carried out all that was asked of them. However, unfortunately, he had recently found out that the aircraft was on a cross-country training exercise and the bombs were unarmed. So, much to their disappointment, there were no medals for bravery forthcoming.

During the days after the crash, Marie, daughter of local fireman, Les Wren, recalls: 'we had two Air Force men billeted on us. They were part of the team to clear and sort out the debris. The two men only had their meals with us as their families lived in North London. After their dinner they would walk up Bell Lane (*now Courser's Road*) to the Bell Public House to try and get a lift or the No.84 Bus to Barnet Underground to get home, but they were always back in time for breakfast. They told us that the plane should never have been up as the crew were not properly dressed in their flying gear. Some had only got shoes on and not flying boots, and it had been shot down by one of our guns.'

Undoubtedly Ewan Taylor had lost a flying boot over Wistlea Crescent. It was amongst three that had fallen from where they had been stored in the aircraft and had been found in various places along the way. Geoff Paine, the war-time Wellington pilot, remarks that they might have preferred to wear shoes if they were not going to fly at a high altitude and at least two of them must have done so, which gave rise to these remarks. As for the belief that the aircraft had been

---

[2] Sadly, in the 1960s, Jack Deuxberry took his own life after being made redundant at the firm where he worked.

shot down by "friendly" fire, this was commonly held by the local community, the airmen's families and some of the air force personnel involved.

John Day, the village bobby, was of the same opinion. His son, John, told me that for weeks afterwards he'd been plagued by local residents handing him bits off the plane including: 'dummy bombs filled with sand', whilst having his time cut out chasing the souvenir hunters. Sadly all his notebooks, which would have supplied so much information, were burnt after his death. Regarding the crash, he always said that the only time the guns at Hatfield brought a plane down was one of our own. Whether this was from inside information or just an opinion we don't know, but it is certainly worth consideration. The Lancaster undoubtedly flew close to de Havillands shortly before it crashed. There had undoubtedly been Bofors guns situated in all four approaches to the airfield (Ellenbrook, Manor Road, Birchwood and Briars Lane) when it came under attack from a German bomber in 1940. However, Bob Robinson, who was an apprentice there, said that although there were AA guns defending the airfield, they were manned by volunteers and only during the day.

The handwriting of the official RAF accident report changes part way through: the first part describing the structural failure of the aircraft and the second, offering a reason. The location is given as 'Warren Hse Farm, Coney Hatch, Sth Mims, Hertfordshire'. The report's author was confusing Colney Heath, Herts, with Colney Hatch, near Finchley, North London, and this mistake has been repeated in reference books. The time of the accident is recorded as 2012 hrs. This seems unlikely, since according to the police inspector at Barnet, he was informed of the accident at 2007 hrs.

The first part of the report reads: 'Crashed caught fire. Investigation by the Accident Investigation Branch. Wing tips failed under down load and wings had failed again near outer engines. Tail had failed – further examination:'. The second part, in a different and almost illegible handwriting continues: 'Accident Investigation Branch. Primary cause. Loss of control in conditions of severe bumpiness and icing resulting in break-up during subsequent dive. Cause of fire not known, but occurred subsequent to structural break up. Bumpy conditions would come unexpectedly – (*two illegible words*) – be no warning of Cumulo-Nimbus.' (*Abbreviations have been written out in full*).

Regarding the break-up of the plane, the report appears to be accurate. The wing tips on either side were undoubtedly the first to go. It would also seem that the two engines that dropped off during the dive were both outer engines, leaving the inner engines to shoot off from the aircraft as it landed on its back. Meanwhile, the tail had failed just before the crash. It's also true that the weather conditions in the report were what would have been expected that night.

Bill Eames, a Stirling pilot, has examined the weather situation with regard to flying conditions. He noted that: 'there had been thunder at Wigsley that afternoon. Such conditions could produce stacked up banks of cloud known as *cumulonimbus*. Such a cloud formation was highly dangerous, even to the most experienced of pilots. It could easily have caused the crash in the fashion described on the accident card. The aircraft was iced up, entering the cloud, the turbulence would have caused the pilot to lose control. After the plane entered into a dive, the wing tips, then the outer engines had broken off as the pilot attempted to level out.'

Weather conditions that night were obviously very bad, hence Leigh Mallory's message of congratulations to his night fighter stations for carrying out their patrols and hence the number of aircraft heading out to Germany that had to turn back due to icing. The latter phenomenon could occur in cumulus nimbus when water droplets in the cloud turned into ice on the aircraft. If severe it could coat the aircraft with thick ice in a few minutes. The only way out was either to climb up as fast as possible above the cloud or to dive full throttle beneath it. Perhaps this had been Ewan's intention when Ernie Ralph described: 'the engines seemed alright, then the engine shut off and then opened up with a terrific roar.' Is this the description of an aircraft battling against icing and making a last desperate attempt to get out of it? Did

Ewan intentionally put L7575 into a dive but the aircraft was unable to stand the strain?

Jimmy Rawnsley ('*Night Fighter*', *Rawnesley & Wright*) encountered a very similar experience when, having returned to base after a visit to the cinema in Andover, he was suddenly drafted to man the gun turret as part of a Blenheim's crew of pilot, radar operator and air gunner.

'It was a filthy night with low cloud, a weeping drizzle, and freezing not far off the ground. We climbed up through the stuff, blind all the way, until at seventeen thousand feet the poor old Blenheim was so solid with ice that it could stagger no higher. So down we came again, with ice flying off the airscrews and splintering off the wings in great chunks.

We bucked and tossed about until I thought the wings would snap off, and we had just passed back over base at five thousand feet when with a final stomach-churning heave, the aircraft went out of control.

The operator and I spent the next few minutes pinned in turn against the roof and the floor, with intervals of floating between the two as weightless as spacemen. I managed to get a hand to my microphone switch and called the pilot, but there was no answer. A pan of ammunition drifted lazily past my face, hesitated, and then wandered off upwards.

Down on the floor I went yet again, ground down by a brutal irresistible force. It was a losing struggle against gravity, and sight and consciousness were beginning to fade. We must have lost a lot of height, and it could not go on much longer. I knew that I must get to the hatch, but I was gradually losing all my external senses, conscious only of my inner thoughts. It was as if I were giving in to the inevitable. There was no particular sense of fear: only a feeling of mild regret that it should all have to end like this.

And then, suddenly, I became aware, even as the outside world seemed to fade, of a small, intensely bright light shining somewhere deep inside me, stirring me to action as the sheer violence of the instinct of self-preservation exerted itself and forced me to get out. Blindly, I groped for the escape hatch, wrenched it off, and threw it away. I shouted and motioned to the operator to get out, but he could not or would not move. Making one last desperate effort, I clawed my way to the edge of the hatch, gathered myself into a ball, and flung myself clear of the aircraft.'

The operator jumped out afterwards, and miraculously, the pilot managed to pull out of the dive and save the aircraft. They were all very lucky to have survived.

Ewan and his friends would have suffered a similar experience as their plane spiralled out of control, but in their case the instinct for self-preservation was not sufficient to save them. Though the weather was certainly conducive to turbulence and icing, as the accident report suggested, there was one facet of the crash the Air Investigation Branch were unable to answer: 'cause of fire unknown'. And, this could throw an entirely different light on the reason for the accident.

At Smallford, Nancy Roberts and her sister had both been sent into the dugout in their garden at Butterwick Farm after the air-raid warning. Their mother, Enid Roberts was out in the garden. Nancy explains:

'My mother used to go out in the garden when the raids were on, to see if the sky was bright orange with light over the London area, as her sister was living in London at the time. She spotted a spark on the wing of one of our planes. Mother watched the spark get larger and larger and know that the plane was burning. The fire was getting worse, and the aircraft then started to spin and fall towards the ground. She then ran into the house and called my father out to see what was happening.'

Her father had then jumped on his bike and cycled off towards the scene. Nancy concluded:

'Mother never said she saw any other aircraft near the downed plane, as we had seen collisions in this area, or

heard of any gunfire at the time she saw the first spark on the aircraft. I have no more recollection of what happened that night, but in the morning mother said that all the airmen had died.'

There's no direct mention in this account of the course the aircraft was taking but we know from the testimony of Joan Francis and Bill Surridge that it was already on fire as it came northwest from the Barnet area towards St Albans. Is it possible that Mrs Roberts could have seen it when they did, or even before: hence the 'spark' that grew into a 'fire'? She was in the habit of looking towards London during an air raid, out of concern for her sister, and L7575 was approaching from that direction. From her account it would seem that she was able to follow the plane right round until it started to 'spin and fall'. But, considering the gloomy weather conditions this seems unlikely. On its final course the Lancaster passed very close to Butterwick Farm and from her description, she undoubtedly would have seen it shortly before it crashed.

But, wherever she first saw it, her testimony proves that the order of events in the accident report are incorrect and, in fact, should be reversed. 'Crashed caught fire', should be "caught fire, crashed" and in the second part of the report: 'fire … occurred subsequent to structural break up' should be the other way round. All the witnesses agreed that from the moment they saw the aircraft breaking through the cloud base, it was on fire. It is true that none of the men who were thrown out of the plane showed any signs of being burnt. This suggests that the fire didn't spread to the fuselage, or at least, the front of the plane, till it struck the ground, but one or both wings were ablaze. The 'ball of flame' Mrs Heffer saw out of her upstairs window was real enough.

One of the de Havilland's apprentices, Bob Robinson, lived at London Colney, less than two miles south-west of Warren Farm. He writes:

'On the night of the crash I was three doors up the road at my Aunt Doris's house in London Colney with my cousins, John, Olive and Gwen, and various other bods, as what went on in those days.

There was an air raid warning at the time, a very black night, I believe, lots of cloud and a bit of desultory A/A fire towards London. We were always a bit bothered on nights when the sirens went early, as the transport café, George's, was only two doors down the road and had a very large lorry park opposite. This was where the drivers used to change over for the night run. Trucks were ferried out of London to our village for the truckers to take over the night drive, always a lot of noise, drivers with torches, lots of shouting, in fact, a very busy scene.

During our conversing in my Aunt's, we suddenly heard an aircraft coming down in what appeared to be a full power dive. We thought instantly he was after the trucks, so John and I shot out of the back door into the garden and looked towards the noise. We then realised it wasn't after London Colney and rushed up the garden, looking towards Colney Heath.

The noise of the dive, really powerful, terminated abruptly and was followed by a "whoof"! This was accompanied by an enormous flash, followed closely by yet another "whoof" as the fuel exploded. This last noise was not a long bang: just as I explained, a "whoof".

In my aunt's back garden it was quite quiet, and at this point we could hear another aircraft going round travelling from left to right, powered by, what I could swear to, Merlin engines: only two, a "Mossie", not another aircraft with four engines. So, we all thought instantly that a "Kraut" had been shot down.

In those days I was very enthusiastic about aircraft and could recognise most things in the sky. We were used to the sound of Merlins, for "Mossies" flew around all the time from de Havillands.'

Bob's description of the plane crashing as an 'enormous flash' and a 'whoof' is very similar to Arthur Allen's 'flash' and a 'wumph' in Chapter 14.

Cycling to work next day, Bob had seen the starboard wing tip 'of a large bomber' on the grass verge just beyond the junction of Smallford Lane with the North Orbital Road but didn't realise till he was informed at de Havillands that it was from a Lancaster. The following day he had gone cycling with his friends and seen the engines in the field opposite Coursers Farm. 'I can remember this as if it happened yesterday. I believe the Lanc was shot down by a night fighter. Aircraft do not come down as this one did and break up during the dive unless they have been badly damaged by cannon fire. Just a theory, but one I believe to this day.'

Bob didn't see the Mosquito, it was above cloud level, but the direction from which it was coming, i.e. 'left to right', could have been from the area where the Lancaster had started its final dive. I asked him whether this was significant but he didn't think so. The "Mossie" could have circled round several times during the interval between the Lancaster crashing and when he heard the Merlins. But he felt certain that the Mosquito must have seen the bomber burning on the ground as it would have been visible for miles around, and that the twin-engine fighter was circling above the area to have a look. Whether the Mosquito was responsible was another matter. Hatfield itself was not an operational air base. Mosquitoes were taken there only for repairs.

The nearest night fighter station was at Hunsdon, about twelve miles away. At this time 157 Mosquito Squadron was based there. The Operations Record Book reported: 'About 18 E/A operated over S.E.England, 8 penetrating as far as London.' 157 Squadron flew five sorties that night. Two were offensive over Germany setting off soon after 7 p.m. They would have been out of England when the crash took place and didn't return till long after. Three were night patrols. F/Sgt Hughes and F/Sgt Graham took off at 7 p.m. and were: 'scrambled under Easthill control. A contact gained and short chase ensued, which ended when A.I. went u/s' (*ORB*). In other words: the radar tracking system in the aircraft broke down. They landed at 8.30 p.m. F/O Whitlock and F/O Hull took off at 6.45 and landed at 9 p.m. The ORB reports: 'scrambled, uneventful'. W/C Kerr and F/O Vas Nunes (Dutch) took off at 7.40 and landed at 8.55 p.m. The ORB simply says: 'uneventful'. If any of these was the Mosquito that Bob heard, the most likely was that of Wing Commander Kerr who took off about twelve miles from the crash site roughly ten minutes before it happened. However, the ORB has nothing more to say. None of the other few fighter stations flying sorties that night were based anywhere near the St Albans area, so it would have been even more of a coincidence if they were in any way involved.

Like Bob Robinson, Jim Butters and his elder brother, John, were mad about aircraft. They had seen the burning Lancaster as it broke through the cloud cover that evening. They had cycled down towards the crash site the following day and on their way, noticed the wing tip near Smallford Station. Jim writes: 'my late brother was employed at the time by de Havilland and remained so until his death in 1966. I joined as an apprentice in 1946 and remained there until retirement in 1993. Both of us were in design.' In fact, Jim eventually became the Chief Airframe Design Engineer for British Aerospace.

From their home at 2, Woodland Drive, on the eastern outskirts of St Albans, they heard the sound of an aircraft approaching and went outside to investigate. The cloud base was too low for them to see anything but they identified from the sound of the four Merlin engines that it was a Lancaster. As they stood at their front gate the Lancaster passed by and the sound of its receding engines was replaced by the quieter twin Hercules radial engines of a Beaufighter closing in at a similar altitude to the bomber. They then heard gunfire. All this was above cloud level so was only identifiable from what they heard. But, not long afterwards, they saw the Lancaster diving through the cloud cover to a low altitude and on fire. Jim writes: 'I would not care to suggest time intervals for the various events, but there was no doubt in our minds at the time that the sound of Beaufighter cannon-fire preceded the Lancaster's descent by a margin consistent with there having been cause and effect.'

As regards the identification of the Beaufighter's engines, to those like Jim Butters and Bob Robinson, the difference was unmistakable. Jimmy Rawnsley ('*Night Fighter*') describes the difference when he changed from Beaufighters to Mosquitoes: 'I was not too happy about the change from air-cooled to liquid-cooled engines, and the ear-splitting racket from the stub exhausts of the Merlins was very tiring after the soothing snore of the Hercules.'

There could be no doubt in Jim's mind that he heard a Beaufighter, or "Whispering Death" as it was nicknamed, firing at the Lancaster. On this point he is unswervingly certain. And, it must be remembered when considering their evidence that these lads were brought up in an area steeped in aircraft tradition, with de Havillands and Handley Page Works just round the corner. They lived and breathed aircraft and to many it was a natural progression from school into the aircraft industry.

The biggest problem, however, is to verify their testimony. There was another squadron at Hunsdon, that October. Squadron 515 had been formed a year earlier from a special Defiant flight that were experimenting with radar jamming equipment. The Defiant's original role had been of a fighter, powered by a single Merlin engine but with a crew of two, pilot and gunner. The latter had to squeeze into a dorsal gun turret armed with four Browning machine guns (though they had experimented at an earlier stage with cannon). It had by this time been phased out as a night fighter and remained in use solely for various support roles. From June 1943 the Squadron was also being supplied with Beaufighters and became: 'involved in radar calibration and searchlight co-operation' (*'Aces High', Shores & Williams*). A page from their ORB from the 10th to the 23rd October proves interesting.

From the 10th-15th October the whole squadron was grounded due to: 'bad weather and low visibility. Nothing further to report for this period'. These days are bracketed together in one entry. Oct 16th: 'The weather improved on this day and practice flying was resumed.' Defiants were flying during the day. Then Pilot F/O D.K.Foster carried out a night flying test from 1445-1600 hrs and dusk landings from 1745-1840 hrs in Beaufighter 3368. Oct 17th: Defiants practised during the day in preparation for a cross-country that night but it was cancelled due to the weather. However, F/O Foster took up the same Beaufighter from 1850-2025 hrs for some night flying. Oct 18th: Defiants practised all day and went out on a cross-country that evening from 2130-2240 hrs. Oct 19th: Defiants up in the morning. Night flying cancelled: 'owing to bad weather and gale warning.' Oct 20th: In the morning, Defiants on cross-countries, and 'A.I.Homings' (i.e. radar tracking) practised in Beaufighter 3368, piloted by F/Sgt Chown. 'The same pilot in this aircraft also carried out night flying test in anticipation of night flying but, owing to weather conditions becoming bad, night flying programme was cancelled.' Oct 21st: 'Local flying carried out during the day and during the evening Defiant aircraft AA378 (Pilot P/O S.Lewis, Gunner W/O G.H.Moon) and Defiant aircraft AA418 (Pilot F/S L.D.Anderson and Gunner F/Sgt Rowe) carried out searchlight co-operation flights from 1830-2010 hours.' Oct 22nd: 'Owing to adverse weather no flying carried out during the morning. Air to sea firing by four Defiant aircraft carried out off Frinton from 1450-1540.' Oct 23rd: 'Practice night flying programme was arranged and night flying test in two Defiant aircraft carried out during the afternoon but owing to low visibility and mist this programme was cancelled.'

For anyone unaware of the significance of what occurred twelve miles away on the night of 22nd October there would be nothing out of the ordinary in this report. But on closer examination it will be noted that on each and every day apart from the 22nd there's a record of what happened in the evening or what was planned for the evening and had to be cancelled owing to bad weather. On the 22nd we are told that there was no flying in the morning due to 'adverse weather'. In the afternoon four Defiants practised air to sea firing off the coast at Frinton. But in the evening: nothing. No mention is made of weather conditions being too poor for flying or planned flights being cancelled: just nothing. It is indeed a strange coincidence that such an omission should occur on the very evening in question.

The Inquest dealt with the immediate cause of the men's deaths. The Doctor stated that none of them had suffered injury before the actual moment of the crash, e.g. there were no bullet wounds. The wider issue of what caused the crash was not considered. There was no enquiry as to whether the aircraft had received any damage from gunfire. The Accident

Report is also silent on this point. As far as the AIB were concerned the crash could be put down to weather conditions and there the matter ended.

Squadron Leader Ted Porter affirmed at the Inquest that the wireless equipment in the aircraft had been checked. There were all sorts of electronic gadgets in these Lancasters. How much was checked, we don't know. One such item of equipment was the IFF Box. "Identification Friend or Foe" worked on radar. It would be switched on by the wireless operator in a bomber returning from a raid, for example, to ensure that it wasn't fired on by Anti Aircraft Batteries. The box would respond to a radar signal sent out from the ground. If it did so, it could be identified as a friendly aircraft. Unfortunately, even if the box was switched on, it didn't always respond.

Another method of identification was by "Colours of the Day". The wireless operator would fire coloured flares from a Very pistol. The colours would be changed on a regular basis and a friendly aircraft could be identified if the correct colours were fired. This would obviously work better in good visibility, which was not the case that night. However, the searchlight batteries involved in the training exercise that evening would have been informed that it was taking place. We don't know where they were situated, or even the route, except that it included the St Albans area.

This raises the important question of why the planned route for this exercise took the aircraft so close to London. Johnny Kirkup's crew, on their final exercise a week earlier, had been sent up towards the Scottish border. London had been targeted by the Luftwaffe for the past week. It seems a strange decision, but one, like so many others, that will remain unanswered.

In the end, we are faced with five possible causes for the crash and assessing the likelihood of each, namely: bad weather, mechanical failure, enemy aircraft fire, ground based anti-aircraft fire or "friendly" aircraft fire. Whilst considering the possibilities it should be remembered that L7575 had been "hammered" over Augsburg the previous year: so much so, that it had at first been declared a write-off. It was never used operationally again and then at the conversion unit had spent two lengthy spells undergoing repairs. Apart from that, Corporal Allan Jones had been sent down to Salisbury on one occasion to repair one of the engines.

It all adds up to an aircraft that would have been more vulnerable to adverse conditions of any kind. This was certainly the case on the night in question. The weather was very bad, and that, basically, was the explanation for the accident given in the official report. The problem lies in its failure to explain the cause of the fire and its inaccuracy when stating that the fire occurred: 'subsequent to structural break up'.

The second possible cause could have been mechanical. Enid Roberts described the 'spark on the wing' that gradually grew in size, but no gunfire at the time she first noticed the spark nor any other aircraft nearby. Could some sort of engine trouble have caused a fire that the pilot was unable to extinguish? Or, as it was such a cloudy night, would she have necessarily seen another aircraft near the bomber? Both Ernie Ralph and Gus Heffer in their statements agree with her that there was no gunfire from the time they first noticed the bomber but unlike her, they both testify that there had been shortly before. In any case, if the problem had been simply mechanical, Tom Green could have transmitted a message to base warning them of the problem, but no message was received.

Could the firing have come from one of the German intruders? There was undoubtedly an air raid alert at the time and one raider had definitely got into the area, dropping a 'high explosive bomb' into a field near Colney Street. Some of the anti-aircraft fire could undoubtedly have been directed at the German bomber, though we don't know when it got to the area. According to my father's diary: 'we had an alert at 7.20 and the all clear at 8.30.' L7575 probably crashed at round about 7.50 or soon after. The two aircraft might have been in the area at the same time but few of the witnesses mentioned another aircraft: just Jim Butters who heard the Beaufighter, Bob Robinson who heard the Mosquito, and David Willson, who, without being very specific, mentioned that there were other aircraft flying around. Unfortunately none of the squadron records of the German aircraft flying to England that night survive.

At an earlier period their night fighters had been following the bomber stream back to Britain and picking our aircraft off as they circled the airfields for landing, but by this time they had changed to attacking ground targets. All their night fighters, even the single seater FW 190, could carry a bomb. The general report that does survive only states that the Luftwaffe 'achieved direct bomb hits on the set target areas'. It doesn't say what these targets were and it doesn't mention shooting down any enemy aircraft. Though their night fighters' armament of cannon would have sliced through a Lancaster had they been given the chance, the type of raids these aircraft were carrying out at this time were designed to rapidly strike at ground targets and withdraw as quickly as possible in order to avoid our night fighters. They were not hunting other aircraft; on the contrary, they were trying to avoid them.

From Ted Stebbing's evidence we get closer to the truth. On the western outskirts of Potters Bar, he described how he heard: 'heavy gunfire close at hand and a plane buzzing around ... silence for a while, then some more gunfire further away, followed by a zooming noise and a bump.' He doesn't specify what type of fire he heard, but Police Inspector Harold Harris in his report on the accident had noted: 'the air raid alert had been sounded and gun fire had been heavy in the district.' As he was based at Barnet, this gunfire could well have been the same as 'the heavy gunfire' Mr Stebbing heard 'close at hand' and would describe the heavy pounding of ground-based anti-aircraft fire. It obviously hit the Lancaster and started the fire that Joan Francis and Bill Surridge observed from Shenley Lodge and Tyttenhanger Farm as the aircraft flew northwest towards St Albans. The debris that Ralph Howell and his friends saw at Tyttenhanger Green was almost certainly the result of the gunfire near Potters Bar. It wasn't sufficient to impede the aircraft's manoeuvrability too much: such as a section of covering off the rear fuselage, leaving a hole through which contents from inside the plane could fall out. It was at Tyttenhanger that the first of three flying boots was discovered and the place in the aircraft for storing odds and ends was most likely to be in the rear fuselage.

With the Lancaster already in such trouble it seems strange that no distress signal was ever received from it. This raises the possibility that the wireless equipment was damaged in the initial gunfire and even perhaps the internal communication system, making contact between crew difficult. Tom Green, the wireless operator, never left the aircraft and wasn't, in fact, found till several days after the crash. Although according to the inquest the doctor examined all the bodies there's no detailed post mortem on him: in fact, only a note added to say that his body was burnt after death. It seems likely that the fire inflicted so much damage that there was little left to examine. The fact that all the others in front of the plane and even the mid-upper gunner were thrown out and Tom wasn't, suggests that he was not with them at the end. Although the doctor stated that none of the men received any injury until the moment of impact, it's difficult to see how he could have known this in the case of such a badly damaged body. Tom might have been killed or severely injured by the initial gunfire.

This had already caused enough damage but there was worse to come. Ted Stebbing observed: 'there was silence for a while, then some more gunfire followed by a zooming noise and a bump.' This could have been the cannon fire from the Beaufighter. The Luftwaffe had no four-engine bombers, so how could such a tragic mistake have occurred? The answer is probably down to two factors: poor visibility due to bad weather conditions making aircraft recognition difficult and, because there was an air raid alert in that area, the strong likelihood that any plane encountered would be hostile. As the Lancaster was already on fire this may also have induced the Beaufighter pilot to think it was hostile. A fleeting glance at an aircraft, likely to be German, might have been sufficient to induce the fighter pilot to fire. Ground stations vectoring the fighter on to contacts were unable to identify the type of aircraft on their radar screens. This could only be done when the fighter crew had made visual contact. It's even possible in this case that a ground station wasn't involved and it was just a chance encounter.

George Archer in Camp Road was a little to the south of Jim Butters. He was outside his factory looking north towards Sandridge when he heard an aerial explosion in that direction shortly before he saw the plane come down. The anonymous correspondent, entitled 'A.N.Other', had been crossing the Barnet Bypass on the junction with Lemsford Road and Green Lanes. He/she writes: 'pitch dark cloudy night when about three aerial explosions took place, believed at the time ack-ack fire. The flaming object came from a northerly direction travelling southerly, more or less on the overall line of the Barnet Bypass.' This was in fact south-westerly and where Ed Kean saw it from Welwyn.

David Willson in Endymion Road, Hatfield, was a little to the southeast of the anonymous writer. He recalls: 'we heard an aircraft flying around on the far side (*the west side*) of de Havillands. We went outside to listen and heard a burst of machine gun fire followed by an explosion. Then, there was a sound like four Spitfires diving followed by a tremendous vibration.' When I asked him whether he heard any other planes, he said he had heard other aircraft around. The 'four Spitfires' were, he explained, the four Merlin engines on the Lancaster and the 'tremendous vibration' was the plane crashing. The 'explosion' or 'explosions', mentioned by three independent witnesses must have been the result of anti-aircraft gunfire from a ground battery or cannon fire from an aircraft inflicted on the Lancaster. In view of the Butters brothers' precise identification of a Beaufighter, it seems most likely that this aircraft was the culprit and the fact that three witnesses heard an explosion indicates that its fire had struck the Lancaster.

In reviewing the testimony of the various witnesses, it's important to stress the evidence of two people dating from the time of the crash. Their memories were not clouded by the passage of time, though it can be seen from their description of events, neither were particularly knowledgeable about aircraft. Ted Stebbing clearly associates guns firing with an aircraft. First it was near at hand and later, further off, 'followed by a zooming noise and a bump'. There was no doubt in his mind: 'It sounded as though a plane had been brought down.' From Ernie Ralph we get the route of the plane as 'it appeared to come northwest and then to north and over towards southeast'. This, basically, describes the flight path, without going into intricate details.

Having established the likely origins of L7575's misfortunes as "friendly fire" from two probable sources and the aircraft's route from the way it appeared to witnesses and debris strewn along its flight path is it possible to deduce the reasons for the pilot's actions and why the aircraft started to break up over Smallford? The sequence of events and technical details that follow are largely at the suggestion of Jim Butters with his knowledge of aerodynamics, local geography and deductions from the testimony of witnesses. However, it must be emphasized that there is not sufficient evidence to qualify this account as any more than speculation, as he would be the first to admit. Unfortunately, after more than sixty years, and the scanty evidence still available, it's probably as close as we shall ever get to what actually happened.

It seems that there was a turning point in the flight schedule that took L7575 into the St Albans area. Eric Williams, the navigator, would have had the necessary maps and might well have been given the chance to study and familiarise himself with them. Weather conditions were atrocious: misty rain, low cloud and poor visibility. Whether they had strayed a little off course we don't know, but they found themselves on the northern outskirts of London during an air raid alert (*see maps in appendices*).

Somewhere near Potters Bar they were hit by fire from an anti-aircraft battery. The likely damage was to one wing, causing a fire, the communications system and the rear fuselage. Tom Green, the wireless operator, might also have been hurt, but in any case, if he did try to send a message, it was not received at base. The top priority now was to get away from the danger zone and Ewan Taylor, the pilot, headed north-west, out of the London area. Meanwhile, attempts were being made to extinguish the fire in the wing, but with little success. Near Tyttenhanger Green, Ewan saw St

Albans ahead of him and swung over to the northeast to avoid the city. In doing so the aircraft shed some debris, though nothing much to impede its manoeuvrability.

It was as they passed close to the north-eastern edge of the city that the Beaufighter attacked. Witnesses heard an explosion, indicating that L7575 had been hit, yet again, by "friendly fire". This might have been the point where Ewan decided that he could continue no further and must look for a place to land his crew safely. The airfield at de Havillands was just over to the east of them. Alternatively, Eric, his navigator might have been trying to head him towards de Havillands after they had first been hit, and in the poor visibility, had strayed a little to the west of the airfield. Whatever the case, Ewan circled round and dived down towards the northern end of the airfield, but at this stage was at too high an altitude to attempt a landing. It should be noted, in passing, that the concrete runway at de Havillands was not built till after the War, so the airfield on such a gloomy night would not have been that easy to see.

He decided to try a landing from the southern end of the airfield, so cut back on a westerly course to St Albans crossing close to Beech Farm, where a small panel from the fuselage was later found. Over St Albans he swung round onto an easterly course, diving to a lower altitude and throttling down to prepare for landing. Attempts to douse the fire had failed. His last hope of saving the crew was to land on the airfield and try to get everybody out of the aircraft as quickly as possible. With the fire spreading, it was a slim chance, but the only one left open to him.

From his angle of approach the ground would start to rise about half a mile from the airfield perimeter. It was just at this point that suddenly, his eye caught the outlines of a wireless transmission mast looming out of the darkness directly ahead, and another to the left of it, close behind. Situated just off Sand Pit Lane (*officially, Oaklands Lane*), there were altogether four w/t masts, each towards a corner of a square-shaped field with a solid brick-built building in the centre: a Post Office radio station. Jim Bacon, the young postal worker from Smallford, recalls that when it had been built, two Scottish steel workers, employed to erect the masts, had lodged at his parents' house. His friend's father worked there and sometimes had to climb the 200 ft masts. The two more southerly ones were taken down soon after the War and the other two, cut down to 100 ft a few years later when the runway at de Havillands was extended. An aerial photograph taken in 1948 confirms the remaining masts at half the original height and that the square bases were about 30 ft across. The aerials were a formidable obstacle placed so near to an airfield. Probably unlit in the wartime blackout, they would have posed a deadly threat to the unwary.

Ewan's immediate reaction was to bank sharply to starboard, opening out to full throttle. It saved him for the moment. They were now on a south-easterly course over the northern outskirts of Smallford heading in the direction of Colney Heath, but in a hard right turn. There were a number of nurseries here with an extensive area under glass. To level off and maintain adequate height, he applied aileron hard left.

It was this manoeuvre that finally sealed their fate. The strain on the port wing of the steep right hand turn then levelling off, bending it, first in one direction and then in the other, together with the structural weakening caused by the fire was too much for L7575. The port wing tip broke off and fell on the post office just north of Smallford Railway Station.

From this point Ewan began to lose control. The loss of the port wing tip would have raised the starboard wing. To correct the rotation he would have instinctively moved the column hard right for the starboard aileron to come up. The resulting download on the starboard wing broke it downwards. The starboard wing tip was later discovered upside down, with the aileron missing, at the junction of Smallford Lane with the main orbital road.

The crew were now in a hopeless position. Any attempt to maintain a shallow approach was impossible as the wings continued to break up. An outer engine came off over the western side of Colney Heath village and the Lancaster began to descend in an uncontrollable spin. It was then only a matter of time, not more than a few seconds, before the end.

There's strong evidence from one of the official witnesses to believe that Ewan throttled down in preparation to land and subsequently had to apply full boost. Ernie Ralph said in his statement to police that: 'the engines seemed all right, then the engine shut off and then opened out with a terrific roar'. He noted that: 'previous to first hearing the plane, there was gunfire in the direction of Harpenden and Luton.' As Ralph was observing the scene from Colney Heath the cannon fire from the Beaufighter would have been exactly in that direction. The w/t masts as the cause of Ewan's failure to land at Hatfield and the start of the aircraft's disintegration is of course a theory, but fits in with what little we know.

Too many odds were stacked against them from the moment they flew off in an ageing plane in bad weather, to their arrival at the scene of an air raid where they were fired upon from the ground and the air, to the final twist of fate as they were forced to change course just when they had the last chance to save themselves. Ewan did his best to keep the aircraft steady but eventually, inevitably, L7575 could take no further punishment. After a terrible beating she fell apart taking her crew with her.

Seven men took off from Wigsley that night on their final training flight. They were never to return. In the service record of F/O Eric Williams, the Navigator, there's a neat line ruled through the entry 'No.467 Squadron 22.10.43', with the word 'CANCELLED' written above it. Below is written: 'Killed on active service. Accident to Aircraft on 22.10.43'.

17.   5320 + 7

'5327 officers and men were killed and a further 3113 injured in RAF training accidents 1939-45' (*'Bomber Command', Max Hastings*). In addition to Ian Hayward's Wellington Crew of five on the afternoon of the 22nd October 1943 (*Chapter 13*), and Ewan Taylor's Lancaster crew of seven that evening, Bomber Command lost a further three aircraft from Heavy Conversion Units during the night. Two of these were Stirlings from HCU 1657 on navigation exercises, taking off from Stradishall. One crashed just before 9 p.m. trying to land at Chipping Warden on three engines and in the process had hit a tree and a couple of roof tops. It seems that because of the poor weather conditions they had mistaken the perimeter track for the runway. Of the crew, four were killed instantly, one died the following day and the two others were injured but survived. Within half an hour the other Stirling crashed near Hereford when it nose-dived into the ground. The crew of nine were all killed. They included P/O Victor Gerrard, on the unit's staff as a navigation instructor, having completed a tour of duty with 90 Squadron. Like Bernard Jobling at Wigsley the previous August (*Chapter 10*), his was yet another example of the perils facing experienced aircrew "resting from ops". Six of the men who died with Gerrard had narrowly escaped injury earlier in the month when their Stirling had swerved out of control on take off, causing the undercarriage to collapse, which wrecked the aircraft. Sadly, their luck deserted them on the night of the 22nd.

It wasn't till the early hours of the following morning that a Halifax from HCU 1664 with a crew of six was preparing to land at Croft, their base, after a night exercise. Suddenly one of the outer engines cut, throwing the aircraft into a steep roll. It crashed into trees killing five of the crew outright. Two local civilians very bravely managed to pull the remaining man away from the burning wreck, but he died four days later. Thus, within twenty-four hours Bomber Command had lost four aircraft from training units, resulting in the deaths of thirty- two men, with a further two, injured.

The closing stages of L7575's life were, sadly, recorded on the Air Ministry movement card. When, on the 24th October 1943, it was written down as 'Category E (Burnt)', i.e. totally destroyed, the tragedy was already two days old. Then, finally, on the 15th November, with the designation 'S.O.C.' (*Struck off Charge*), this brave but prematurely old Lancaster disappeared from the RAF's inventory of aircraft and entered into the pages of history. It had taken a terrible bashing and only succumbed when it simply couldn't take any more.

A week after the crash twelve year old David Willson from Hatfield had gone down after school with one of his classmates to see his grandfather in Colney Heath. Having walked from Smallford he crossed the Orbital Road. 'We went down past the church to the pumping station where my grandfather worked, then took the footpath onto the common, through the wood and into the corn field. The wrecked plane still lay there in the distance but we were soon spotted by guards who shouted at us to keep away. What we did see, though, lying in the field about three to four hundred yards from the plane in the direction of the waterworks, was the control column, still attached to a section of the cockpit floor and part of the instrument panel. About fifty yards from this was a large oxygen cylinder, about eighteen inches in diameter and four feet long.' How the control column had got so far from the main wreckage is a mystery. When the aircraft hit the field it had come to rest on its back. Perhaps this small section of the cockpit had been hacked away by the rescuers trying to get into where Tom's body was found in the front of the plane.[3]

Even after the main bulk of wreckage had been cleared, bits and pieces kept turning up. Months after the crash, Bill Surridge working on Tyttenhanger Farm had a fright. 'I was

---

[3] A year later, in October 1944, David Willson was blinded and nine people, including his eighteen-month-old brother, were killed, when a V1 flying bomb exploded near their home.

cultivating potatoes when the large spade lugs on the tractor dug up what I took to be a small bomb. I quickly dived for cover waiting at any moment for the thing to explode. When nothing happened I had a closer look and it turned out to be an oxygen cylinder about a foot to eighteen inches long.' When tractors disturbed the ground close to Warren Farm, fragments of metal kept appearing for many years after the War. In the 1970s a wireless and cooler system were dredged up from the River Colne, where, like rusty old prams and supermarket trolleys they had probably been dumped.

Within a month of the crash all available Lancasters were needed for operational units and Wigsley converted to Stirling IIIs. After the War the airfield was still used as a satellite for Swinderby until it was finally de-requisitioned on the 1st July 1958.

Corporal Allan Jones, on the wartime groundcrew there, had married a local girl and settled in the nearby village of Saxilby. His son Malcolm remembers Wigsley in the late 1950s: 'I was a very keen cyclist in my youth and occasionally would cycle over to Wigsley and have a race down the concrete runway with my friends. There was still a hangar at the southwest end and some dispersal huts in the trees to the northwest. If you knew where to go in the pine woods you could find a grave to a dog that obviously used to belong to someone on the aerodrome. Occasionally the drome would be closed to the public if it was used for circuits and bumps for trainers out of Swinderby. Following decommissioning it reverted to agricultural use and the road across the runway from Spalford to Harby was made permanent.'

He recollects in recent years: 'When driving from the south to visit my parents in Saxilby, I would sometimes divert off the main road and go across country past the old control tower. Over the years it has become vandalised, but is still there as an eerie monument to all those souls from the war years that are mostly now forgotten (*see photograph of Wigsley taken in 2004*). The last time I passed by was on the way to my father's funeral and I shed a few tears in memory.'

Looking at the pitiful state of the control tower and the bleak landscape around it, it's difficult to believe that in 1943 this was a busy airfield. On Saturday the 23rd October that year, my father, still unaware of what had happened to Tom, triumphantly announced in his diary: 'This is the anniversary of the great Battle of El Alamein which began at 9.40. The 8th Army has progressed 2,500 miles since then.'

It was a tough and bloody struggle up the spine of Italy. The Allies were winning the War on all fronts, both East and West, but it would be many months before it was over and in that time many loved ones would be lost. Despite the sorrow that every family felt when personal tragedy affected them there was that wartime spirit of "carry on regardless" that encouraged most to do what was required of them, to rise to the occasion in their own particular way.

To young Jim Bacon, a Post Office messenger at St Albans, there was from time to time a stark reminder of the reality of War. For, to this fifteen-year-old and his workmates was given the unenviable task of bearing the bad tidings: that dreaded knock on the door. He remembers: 'I would report for duty at St Albans Post Office and then we boys waited for our first job. A message would come through on the teleprinter in the adjoining room and the girl would pass it through the hatch to our supervisor. There was a strict order of seniority and it was always the most junior who got the first job, and so on. The address and messenger's name were recorded in a book and if it was my turn, off I went. It was what we called the "Government priority" telegrams that we dreaded. They came in a buff envelope with a blue stripe down the left side. These telegrams were always bad news: either someone missing, killed or a prisoner of war. I distinctly remember a woman in Park Street: that stunned look on her face as she read the telegram. It really brought the War home to me.'

My father noted in his diary: 'I don't like War Office telegrams. They seem so cold blooded, with their specification of two 3rd Class return fares to their cemetery, or use of coffin, £5, if buried locally.' His diary is a mixture of family matters and the latest news on the war front. The day of Tom's funeral was approaching. Thursday 28th Oct. 'Ordered a wreath for Tom. The RAF are sending a representative to the funeral. The Russians are outside Krivoy Rog. Friday 29th Oct. 'Freda (*my mother*) was in the town this afternoon and saw Feltham's (*the undertaker's*) hearse coming from Godalming Station with Tom's body under the Union Jack – the flag of flags. It upset her, but I'm glad one of us saw it. The Germans are sending big reinforcements to try and hold Krivoy Rog. Road accidents in September, 455 killed, 10,000 injured.' Saturday 30th Oct. 'Bought two pairs of pyjamas, cost £3/11/-d (*£3.55p*). Had a haircut. Had an alert this evening, went on patrol. Went to Mrs George about her light. Saw a man going in who denied they had any light... the light went out. Heard no gunfire or bombs. There is a terrific battle going on for Krivoi Rog where the Germans have thrown in reserves.' Sunday 31st Oct. 'Dull and a little drizzle. Cleaned the pram today. May (*Tom's mother*) phoned today to say there was a note on Tom's coffin – not to be opened. A few raiders came in over the South East Coast yesterday evening and some reached the London Area. Some damage and a few casualties. Two were brought down, both by Mosquitoes. We had an alert at 10 p.m., which lasted till 11. There were red and green flares – nine of them – to the South and gunfire over East London and also due North of us. North West there was a bright red glow, which lasted only a second.' Monday 1st Nov. 'A day of drizzle. Tom was buried this afternoon. I noted that some people were very respectful when his coffin went past with the Union Jack, but there were many who took no notice. They might respect those who die for them. Mr Knight gave an address. All is well with Tom. Chas and May were very brave and very quiet. I am truly grieved for them but one thing is sure. They will see him again.'

Like Tom, the Australian, Bruce Davies, was an only child. His mother, Effie, was inconsolable. In a letter to his father's cousin John Wilson, the teacher at Charterhouse School, dated 19th March 1944, his father, Walford, wrote: 'Dad has passed on to me your air graph letter of Feb 21st and I feel that I must write and thank you personally for the kind things you have said of our son and your kindness to him when he visited you. He was our only son and his death has been a terrible blow. In one of his last letters he spoke of his visit to you and was full of praise and admiration of you all, and he had hoped to visit you many times more. We received very little information from the RAAF and all we know is that his plane crashed at Sth Mimms, Coney Hatch, "accidentally", and that he was buried in Brookwood Cemetery. I have written to his C.O. at Wigsley for further details but so far have heard nothing.'

The RAAF have repeated the error on the accident card, confusing Colney Hatch, near Finchley, North London, with Colney Heath, near St Albans. The inverted commas round the word 'accidentally' are Walford's. He obviously thought that there was more to it than the authorities were prepared to admit. As this letter was written nearly five months after the event and he had still received no satisfaction there was absolutely no chance of him getting any further with his enquiries.

Meanwhile, there were not seven, but eight families directly affected by the crash, for it effectively claimed one civilian life. Just a month later, on the 22nd November, Mrs Elizabeth Heffer at the farmhouse died. She never recovered from the shock of what she had seen that night. In the words of her daughter, Phyllis: 'my biggest regret being that she didn't see my two brothers come home from the Army or any of us married, so missing out on her grandchildren.'

Within ten months of the crash, the man who had authorised the flight was also dead. His spell at the Conversion Unit had only been a brief respite from operations. Squadron Leader Ted Porter was soon to gain his promotion to Wing Commander. Des Evans, an LAC who serviced his Lancaster at Coningsby remembers him as: 'a wonderful caring man. Courteous, friendly, helpful, he never used his rank. Before the War, a man dedicated to peace, he was against war, until his sister, to whom he was very close, was killed in a very early raid on London. She was a nurse. He enlisted straight away. He led No.9 Squadron as Master Bomber on all the Berlin Raids.'

Jim Logan and Bill Pearson, who had lost their pilot, Johnny Kirkup, on a second dickey trip to Kassel, the same night that Ewan and crew lost their lives, eventually found themselves as part of Ted Porter's crew. They transferred to 97

Squadron in June 1944. Jim remembers: 'Our last two trips with him were in daylight to France on the 1st and 3rd August. Not only did he possess excellent pilot skills but certainly had all the dedication and leadership qualities to carry out the controlling duties to ensure that the bombs fell on the assigned targets and not on the civilian population'.

The crew went on leave but Ted Porter was called back early. On 16th August 461 bombers were sent on a raid to Stettin during which two squadrons, 97 and 83, were to lay mines (known in RAF parlance as "gardening") along the Swinemunde Canal. It was an extremely hazardous low-level operation and Guy Gibson, who led the raid on the Dams the previous year, was at the briefing to give advice. As Jim, Bill and the others were on leave, Ted Porter had to pick a scratch crew. He was the Master Bomber and was assigned to mark the middle of the canal. Caught in a dense knot of searchlights, he flew into a wall of flak with no chance of survival. Max Hastings (*Bomber Command*) continues: 'with an unshakeable calm that every crew listening remembered for the rest of their lives, he said on the R/T: "I'm afraid we have had it. I shall have to leave you now. Bailing out. Good luck everybody". But they were too low for parachutes.'

By a sheer stroke of luck, Jim and Bill had escaped death, but they were soon to part company. On the 29th August, Bill was assigned as an additional eighth member of a Pathfinder crew from 83 Squadron. Their pilot, Squadron Leader E.N.M. Sparks, had only just returned to operational flying having been shot down over France the previous May, evaded capture and found his way back to England. Their Lancaster was to be one of the first to fly in low and mark the target, and for pinpoint accuracy, this required two bomb aimers. Their destination was Königsberg and Bill had just successfully dropped a marker on the railway yards when their Lancaster was hit by flak as they were leaving the target area. Both port engines were put out of action and three of the crew killed. The other five, including the pilot and Bill, baled out safely.

Bill landed heavily on a cobbled road, badly spraining a leg. He managed to roll into a potato patch behind a house, but was immediately surrounded and taken to a barn nearby.

Later he was marched through a crowd who would have lynched him had he not been saved by a Luftwaffe officer who got additional guards to escort him to the local lockup. He writes: 'I could have kissed that Luftwaffe officer; he saved my life.' Bill was, indeed, lucky. Over the course of the War, German civilians killed about 350 British aircrew after they had bailed out. Bill spent the rest of the War in Stalag Luft 1 and was liberated a year later by the advancing Russian army. Jim successfully completed two tours (45 ops) and returned to Canada in February 1945.

Bert Cole, whose crew had been shot down on the 10th August 1943, was another lucky survivor. In this case all the crew parachuted to safety but were soon captured and were in a sorry state by the end of the War. His POW diet had reduced Bert to eight stone. Some fifteen years later, he and his wife paid a visit to Fritwell Manor where he had been billeted when training at Upper Heyford. 'There was a woman hoeing a flower border in the garden. She turned towards us. "Can I help you", she said. I instantly recognised her, and recalled that embarrassing episode in the canteen and how she had read our palms. "I remember you", she said. And then I reminded her of her words all those years ago: "You will survive many crashes and difficulties and you will be away for a long time but will survive it all safely". All she foretold had come true. I had not realised at the time that she was the Lady of the Manor. A wonderful person.'

Not all were as fortunate as Bert and his mates. Ernest Deverill who had flown L7575 so gallantly in the Augsburg Raid only outlived Ewan and crew by a few weeks. He was one of the 127 aircrew killed by the fog on the night of 16th December 1943, forever afterwards known in Bomber Command as "Black Thursday". 483 Lancasters had set out for Berlin. Twenty-five were lost over the target but the worst was yet to come. The remaining force struggled back in dense fog. When they crossed the English coast it was still as thick as ever. Bombers were running out of fuel after the lengthy haul to Berlin, some damaged, groping around in zero visibility, desperately trying to find an airfield, any airfield, to set their wheels down. Twenty-nine aircraft didn't make it. Worst hit was 97 Squadron. Seven were lost, amongst them Deverill's.

It was 12.51 a.m. He had been airborne for over eight hours and found his way to Graveley, one of the Squadron's bases, where the runways were lit with 'FIDO' (Fog Investigation and Dispersal Operation). The runway was lined with pipes pierced with narrow holes at regular intervals. When petrol was pumped through the pipes, a fine spray spurted through each of the holes. Jennie Gray, in her book, 'Fire by Night', explains: 'a man manually set alight the first burner then ran like hell when it ignited with a whoosh. The heat dispersed the fog and cloud, and the glow of the flames provided a flare path.' This system had just recently been introduced and at the time there were only three airfields over the whole country where it had been installed. Graveley, six miles from 97 Squadron's main base at Bourn had been the chief experimental site.

Deverill joined a queue of Lancasters all short of fuel and needing to land. He was instructed to divert to Wyton where conditions were supposed to be better, but he was soon on his way back to Graveley. He called up Control: 'There's no future at Wyton, can I have a crack at your Fido?'

'He approached almost at right angles to the runway. Just as it looked as if he was going to touch down, he opened up and then his engines cut and he crashed into the bomb dump and burst into flames' (*Flying Control Historical Record – Graveley*). Rescue services managed to stop the fire getting to the dump, but when they finally got into the Lancaster only the mid-upper gunner was alive. He was immediately taken to Ely Hospital with compound fractures and second degree burns.

Realising at the last moment that his approach was wrong, he had run out of fuel just as he was about to try another landing. It must be noted here that those who died with him were not the same aircrew that accompanied him on the raid to Augsburg, some of whom undoubtedly survived the War. Since Augsburg, Squadron Leader Ernest Deverill had won a second DFC and was posthumously awarded the AFC. He was buried near his home in Norfolk.

Ewan Taylor RAAF lies in the large military cemetery at Brookwood, near Woking in Surrey next to his Australian comrade, Bruce Davies. The five RAF men in his crew were all taken to their home towns. Eric Williams lies in the City of London Cemetery, very close to his home in Manor Park. Eddie Stock was buried in Islington Cemetery, much grieved by his father and only sister who had grown so close to him after the death of their mother.

The coffin of Albert Rooks was lost on a railway siding somewhere between St Albans and Leeds. His younger sister, Mabel, thirteen at the time, remembers: 'The funeral had already been arranged and they had to postpone it till the next day. Albert's coffin lay in the front room covered in flowers. To this day, whenever I catch the scent of flowers, it always reminds me. There was a notice on the coffin that it was not to be opened and Mother couldn't bring herself to believe that he was really in there. It was a big funeral. The street was full of people as his coffin was carried to the church.' Albert's girlfriend, who had planned to break off her engagement to her soldier fiancé when he returned from abroad, changed her mind and married him. Mabel remembers going to their wedding and that they emigrated to Vancouver Island, Canada.

Despite its remote location, the funeral of John Thwaite was likewise well attended. The little lane up to Newlands Church in the Lake District was crowded with cars. There is an obituary in the Above Derwent Newsletter published at the time and quoted in Susan Grant's book, 'The Story of the Newlands Valley'. It describes him as: 'a fine type of young Englishman – six feet two inches in height and popular with all who knew him. He had flown over Braithwaite just a few nights earlier, and wrote to his father saying he hoped he hadn't disturbed his sleep! The writer tells of the many sympathisers who had made the journey on foot to pay their last tributes, of the coffin draped with the Union Jack, and the service conducted by the Rev. Steele-Smith and the Rev. H. Crossland. He was laid to rest beside his mother in the peaceful valley of Newlands on a lovely October day. We extend our sympathy to his father Mr. Fisher Thwaite and to his brother,

Bill.' Fate had indeed dealt several cruel blows to Fisher Thwaite with the death of his first and second wives followed by one of his two sons.

John Hume, who was at Keswick School with John Thwaite, writes: 'John's grave, surmounted by a military headstone is in Newlands Churchyard, one of the loveliest settings in the Lake District, where among its crags, buzzards spiral and peregrines plummet on passing prey. Frequently I walk past the church and can see his headstone from the lane, and invariably it sets off a train of thought; the memorial at Kohima: "When you go home tell them of us and say, for your tomorrow we gave our today". Was the world mad? Is it any better now? Haven't they learnt anything?'

In the local newsletter, Florence Robinson, a relative of the Thwaites, contributed a short poem (reproduced opposite) that, apart from its allusions to the Lake District, would be a fitting tribute to any of the seven men who died on Colney Heath in the cause of freedom and independence of our country, that autumn night of 1943.

'He came to say "Good-bye," and no one heard.
He gazed from Skiddaw's heights, but nothing stirred;
We, all unknowing, slumbered, while he passed
Along his starry way – then we at last
Awoke to find the one we loved had gone
To that far bourne whence all must tread alone.

But we shall not forget the boy we knew,
The man who, keen to serve, gave life, – his due
That we against the common foe, might win
The long-fought fight; – no thought of self crept in,
Or fame or glory honours to be won,
Only of duty, – duty nobly done.

Once more he came; we followed where he led;
Our grief and flowers revealed the thoughts unsaid.
And so we leave him there, where lonely hills
Stand guard in silence, and where murmuring rills
Flow softly by, and shadows gently creep.
Dip in salute! An airman lies asleep.'

Ewan Taylor, Eric Williams, John Thwaite, Albert Rooks, Thomas Green, Edward Stock and Bruce Davies were seven of the 5327 airmen who gave their lives in training accidents during the Second World War.

This was their story.

~ End ~

APPENDICES

APPENDIX 1: POSITION OF WITNESSES

This sketch map opposite shows the speculated final flight path of Lancaster L7575 (approx scale: 1 inch to the mile)

Position of witnesses who saw
or heard the Lancaster that night:

A. Ted Stebbing
B. Joan Francis
C. The Varty Brothers, Bill Surridge
D. The Butters Brothers
E. anonymous
F. Ed Kean
G. Derry Pickering
H. Jack Last
I. Peggy Phillips
J. The Canfield Brothers
K. Jim Wild, Harry Harrop
L. The Bush Sisters, Bob Arnold, Ernie Ralph
M. The Heffer Family
N. Arthur Allen
O. Enid Roberts & Family
P. Brian Hayward, Alex Whiffen
Q. David Willson
R. George Archer
S. David Ansell, Ralph Howell, Bob Robinson

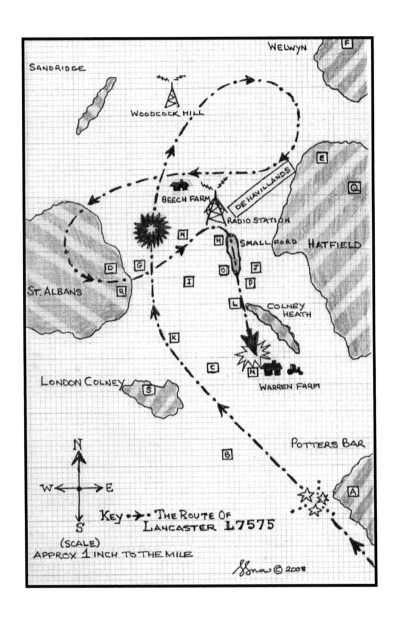

APPENDIX 2: DISTRIBUTION OF DEBRIS

The map shown opposite (approx 2.5 inches to the mile) shows the speculated flight path of the Lancaster as it came north-west from Potters Bar passing to the east of St Albans. Then, after turning in a figure of eight, it re-enters the map. 'X' marks the point where it finally crashed. Figures '1' to '7' show debris that dropped from the aircraft during flight, and '8' to '9' that flew off the plane when it struck the ground.

1) Debris including a flying boot in a field near Tyttenhanger Green

2) Flying boot found by Jack Last whilst poaching rabbits in Sear & Carter's Nursery the following morning.

3) Port wing tip fell on Smallford Post Office

4) Debris at gravel pits just south of Smallford Station

5) Starboard wing tip by junction of Smallford Lane with North Orbital Road

6) Engine on main street of Colney Heath, wing section, pilot's flying boot and other debris nearby

7) Engine at top of orchard, Warren Farm

8) Engine by boundary of field with the heath

9) Engine up against hedge lining Coursers Road close to Coursers Farm

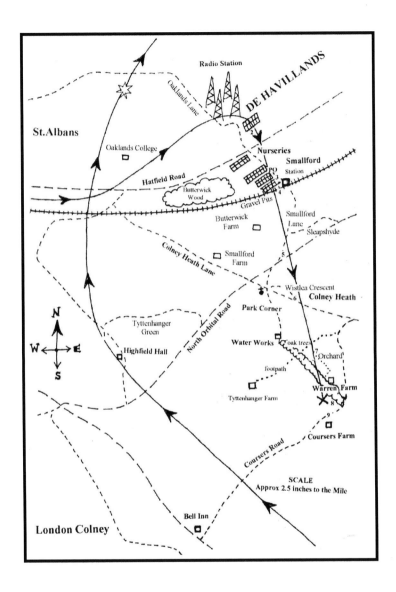

APPENDIX 3: DOCTOR'S STATEMENT

Full Transcription of Doctor's Statement to the Police, 25-10-1943

Statement of:
Ronald Edmund Wilson
54 Holywell Hill
St Albans

Police Station,
Barnet
25th October 1943

Who saith:- I am a fully qualified medical practitioner and reside at 54 Holywell Hill, St Albans. At 8.50 pm on Oct 22nd 1943 I was taken by the St Albans City Police Ambulance to the site of an air crash at Colney Heath where I saw the bodies of four men of the air crew. I subsequently examined them in more detail at the·St Albans City Mortuary on the morning of Oct 23rd, and also the bodies of two more of the same crew on the morning of Oct 24th. All six men had sustained extensive injuries of great severity, such as would be caused by an air crash.

Thwaites[4] – Comminuted fractures of the skull, jaw and pelvis. The left collar bone was broken. There was a deep cut across the right wrist and severe abrasions in the groin.

Taylor – Severe injuries to the skull and brain, most severe on the left side. The left thigh pulped. Pelvis extensively fractured. Right thigh broken. Right arm and right ribs broken. Deep cuts above the right knee and injuries to the left groin.

Stock – The left vault of the skull and the jaw fractured, also the left thigh, pelvis, right leg, left forearm, right arm, and ribs on both sides.

---

[4] 'Thwaites' should be Thwaite.

Rooks – Multiple fractures of the pelvis, left thigh, right hip, all ribs right and left side, left side of nose.

Davies – Head showed severe destruction from a transverse blow across the face, probably from machinery. A deep transverse cut across the front of the neck. Left arm fractured near the elbow and the right elbow smashed. In addition, the right side of the body was severely burnt. Both legs were charred to an ash below the knee and both feet missing by destruction of fire.

Williams – The whole body and head shortened by the severe compression due to a vertical fall, involving severe fractures to the skull, bones of the face, shoulder girdle, all ribs, pelvis, right arm and forearm, left forearm, both thighs and right leg.

The injuries in each case were such as would have caused instant death (and this applies equally to Davies[5], whose body was burnt after death). There was a noticeable similarity in the injuries of Thwaites, Taylor, Stock and Rooks. The latter had not sustained the severe skull injuries, but his body lay beside a thick branch of a tree, which appeared to have been torn off by his fall.

---

[5] After the word 'Davies', '& Green' was added in ink to the typewritten statement, because Green's body wasn't found till later. There's no written evidence of a post mortem on his body.

BIBLIOGRAPHY

Books

The Records of the Royal Air Force – Eunice Wilson

Bomber Command – Max Hastings

Bomber Boys – Kevin Wilson

Bomber Crew – Taylor & Davidson

Bomber Groups at War – Chay Bowyer

Royal Air Force Bomber Command Losses of World War 2 – William Chorley

Royal Air Force Fighter Command Losses of World War 2 – William Chorley

R.A.F. Losses, Heavy Conversion & Miscellaneous Units – William Chorley

The Lancaster Story – Peter Jacobs

Avro Lancaster, The Definitive Record – Harry Holmes

The Avro Lancaster – Francis Mason

Lancaster at War 2 – Garbett & Goulding

Royal Air Force Flying Training & Support Units – Ray Sturtivant

Luck and a Lancaster – Harry Yates

Only Birds and Fools – Norman Ashton

Night Fighter – Rawnsley & Wright

Rear Gunner – John Beede

Fire by Night – Jennie Gray

Aces High – Shores & Williams

Action Stations 2 – Bruce Barrymore Halpenny

Diary of a Decade – Edward Stebbing

The Story of the Newlands Valley – Susan Grant

Newspapers, Periodicals, etc

Daily Telegraph

Aeroplane Monthly (Michael Oakey & Mike Hooks)

Intercom (Ron Gadd)

Herts Advertiser (Beryl Carrington & John Manning)

St Albans & Harpenden Review (Alex Lewis)

Welwyn & Hatfield Times (Terry Mitchinson)

Eastern Courier, Adelaide

Yorkshire Evening Post

Hornsey Journal

Cumberland & Westmorland Herald

Above Derwent Newsletter

RECORDS

H.Q. Bomber Command Reports on Heavy Conversion Units

RAF Squadron Operations Record Books

Metropolitan Police Records

Ships' Passenger Lists

RAF Service Records

RAAF Service Records

Aircrew Log Books

Flying Control Historical Record – Graveley

Meteorological Office Weather Reports

Flugzeugunfälle und Verluste bei den Fl. Verbänden

Eingegangene Meldungen Genst. Luftwaffe Während des 22.10.43

Die Berichte des Oberkommandos der Wehrmacht

Kriegstagebuch der Seekriegsleitung

Hertfordshire County Council Air Raids Precautions Department Reports

Statements of Witnesses at Barnet Police Station

Officers' Reports to Coroner, County of Hertford

Signed Transcripts of Evidence at Inquest

Post Mortems, St Albans City Mortuary

Census Returns, England & Wales

Diary of A.W. Green